The CRYSTAL WISDOM *of* COLORS

BOOK TWO IN THE CRYSTAL WISDOM SERIES

UNVEILING THE HEALING COLORS OF GEMSTONES

SHANNON MARIE

ADULARIA PRESS | HOUSTON, TX

Adularia Press
Houston, TX, USA

Copyright © Shannon Marie, 2021

All rights reserved. No part of this book may be reproduced in any form without permission in writing from the author. Reviewers may quote brief passages in reviews.

Published 2021

Cover and Interior Design by Chris Molè Design

Library of Congress Control Number: 2021914970

ISBN: 978-1-7370282-4-6 (paperback)
ISBN: 978-1-7370282-3-9 (ebook)
ISBN: 978-1-7370282-5-3 (hardcover)

DISCLAIMER

No part of this publication may be reproduced or transmitted in any form or by any means, mechanical or electronic, including photocopying or recording, or by any information storage and retrieval system, or transmitted by email, without permission in writing from the author.

Neither the author nor the publisher assumes any responsibility for errors, omissions, or contrary interpretations of the subject matter within.

The information in this book is no way intended to replace medical care. The reader should still consult their physician or therapist for medical and psychological advice and treatment. Each individual reader is solely responsible for their own healthcare decisions.

*This book is dedicated to
my fellow Wisdom Seekers
and those who have joined me
on the Crystal Wisdom path.*

CONTENTS

Introduction xii

PART 1 – SETTING THE FOUNDATION

Chapter 1: Discovering the Wisdom of Colors 1

Chapter 2: My Color Journey 7

Chapter 3: How to Use this Book 15
   Setting the Foundation 15
   Diving into Color Wisdom 16
   The Practice of Journaling 17
   Sending and Receiving Hands 18
   Additional Notes 19

Chapter 4: How Does Crystal Wisdom Work? 21
   What Is Crystal Wisdom? 21
   What Is Inner Wisdom? 22
   Hearing Your Inner Wisdom 24
   The Wisdom Properties of Gemstones 25
   Using Gemstones to Hear Inner Wisdom 26
   Actively Channeling Crystal Wisdom to Make Change 27
   Crystal Wisdom Combined with Color Wisdom 29

PART TWO – BUILDING YOUR CRYSTAL COLOR PRACTICE

Chapter 5: How Do Crystal Colors Affect Us? 33
   Color Psychology: Color Influence on Emotion and Mind 34
   Chromotherapy: Color Influence on the Body 37
   Chakras and Feng Shui: Color Influence on Energy 40

Chapter 6: Finding Your Wisdom Colors 45
   What Is Comforting to You? 46
   What Are Your Color Preferences? 46
   What Colors Are Repeatedly Arising? 48
   Where Are Synchronicities with Color Occurring? 50

What Colors Do You Choose for Artwork? 51

Chapter 7: Adding Color to Your Crystal Wisdom Practice............53
  Choosing Your Guardian Gemstones...................................53
  Sitting with Your Crystal Color..54
  Creating Your Meditation Space 55
  Learning the Meditation Posture 56
  Sitting with Your Gemstones...58
  Consistent Journaling 58
  Sit with Your Color to Uncover Its Wisdom 59
  Daily and Spontaneous Practices 60

PART 3 – THE WISDOM OF THE COLOR FAMILIES

Chapter 8: BLACK GEMSTONES | PROTECTION 67
  Black Gemstones Help You Cultivate More...
    Grounding 67
    Protection 69
    Comfort..70
  Signs You Need More BLACK Gemstone Energy 71
  Black Gemstones for Protection 72
  Gemstone Meditation for Protection 74

Chapter 9: RED GEMSTONES | ENERGY 79
  Red Gemstones Help You Cultivate More...
    Energy to Live 80
    Energy to Handle Survival Threats 80
    Energy That Ignites Passion 82
  Signs You Need More RED Gemstone Energy........................83
  Red Gemstones for Energy Maintenance...............................84
  Gemstone Meditation for Energy Maintenance 87

Chapter 10: ORANGE GEMSTONES | CREATION 93
  Orange Gemstones Help You Cultivate More...
    Sense of Beauty and Joy 94
    Inspiration and the Ability to Create...............................95

>   The Environment to Reproduce 96
>   Signs You Need More ORANGE Gemstone Energy 97
>   Orange Gemstones for Creation 98
>   Gemstone Meditation for Creation 101

Chapter 11: BROWN GEMSTONES | GROWTH 107
>   Brown Gemstones Help You Cultivate More...
>>   Acceptance of This Life as a Human 108
>>   Responsibility and Financial Stability 108
>>   A Nurturing Environment to Develop 109
>   Signs You Need More BROWN Gemstone Energy 110
>   Brown Gemstones for Growth and Development 110
>   Gemstone Meditation for Growth and Development................. 113

Chapter 12: YELLOW GEMSTONES | CONFIDENCE 119
>   Yellow Gemstones Help You Cultivate More...
>>   Confidence..120
>>   Personal Power 121
>>   Motivation 122
>   Signs You Need More YELLOW Gemstone Energy.................... 123
>   Yellow Gemstones for Confidence 124
>   Gemstone Meditation for Confidence...126

Chapter 13: GREEN GEMSTONES | HEALING 131
>   Green Gemstones Help You Cultivate More...
>>   Healing 132
>>   Compassion... 133
>>   Patience and Harmony... 133
>   Signs You Need More GREEN Gemstone Energy 134
>   Green Gemstones for Healing.. 135
>   Gemstone Meditation for Healing 138

Chapter 14: PINK GEMSTONES | LOVE..143
>   Pink Gemstones Help You Cultivate More...
>>   Unconditional Love..144
>>   Self-Acceptance 145

Forgiveness 145
Signs You Need More PINK Gemstone Energy 147
Pink Gemstones for Love 147
Gemstone Meditation for Love 150

Chapter 15: BLUE GEMSTONES | AUTHENTICITY 155
Blue Gemstones Help You Cultivate More...
    Truth 156
    Authenticity 157
    Communication 158
Signs You Need More BLUE Gemstone Energy 159
Blue Gemstones for Authenticity 160
Gemstone Meditation for Authenticity 162

Chapter 16: LIGHT BLUE GEMSTONES | SPIRITUAL EXPANSION 165
Light Blue Gemstones Help You Cultivate More...
    Expansion 168
    Freedom 168
    Connection to Spirit 170
Signs You Need More LIGHT BLUE Gemstone Energy 170
Blue Gemstones for Spiritual Expansion 171
Gemstone Meditation for Spiritual Expansion 174

Chapter 17: GREY GEMSTONES | TRANSFORMATION 179
Grey Gemstones Help You Cultivate More...
    Transformation 180
    Acceptance 180
    Manifestation 181
Signs You Need More GREY Gemstone Energy 182
Grey Gemstones for Transformation 185
Gemstone Meditation for Transformation 189

Chapter 18: PURPLE GEMSTONES | INTUITION 191
Purple Gemstones Help You Cultivate More...
    Intuition 192

Inner Wisdom..193
Practical Wisdom..193
Signs You Need More PURPLE Gemstone Energy......................195
Purple Gemstones for Awakening Intuition..................................195
Gemstone Meditation for Awakening Intuition 198

Chapter 19: WHITE GEMSTONES | CLEANSING 203
White Gemstones Help You Cultivate More...
Cleansing 203
Purity...204
Peace 205
Signs You Need More WHITE Gemstone Energy 206
White Gemstones for Cleansing 207
Gemstone Meditation for Cleansing..209

Chapter 20: CLEAR GEMSTONES | ENERGY BODY 215
Clear Gemstones Help You Cultivate More...
Energy Amplification 215
Energetic Health...214
Being as One.. 217
Signs You Need More CLEAR Gemstone Energy.......................218
Clear Gemstones for Amplifying Energy 219
Gemstone Meditation for Energy Amplification 221

Chapter 21: Evolving Your Crystal Color Practice...........................225
Practice Regularly 225
Review Your Journal Notes.. 227
Revisit the Color Chapters 229
Embrace the Beauty and Wisdom of Colors...............................229

Chapter 22: Wrapping up 231
Healing Colors Glossary... 233
References..236
About the Author...239
Acknowledgments..240
Thank You!..241

INTRODUCTION

I INVITE YOU TO LOOK UP, TAKE A MOMENT, and notice how many colors you see around you. We are part of a never-ending mosaic of color, transforming in every instant with the change of scenery, light, and direction of our gaze. The reflection of these colors envelopes us, seeping into our eyes and skin. We make intentional choices about which colors to surround ourselves with, whether it be through our choices in clothing, accessories, wall color, or cars. Many people have strong color preferences. This attraction extends to our choice of gemstones as well.

Through my own work with gems, I have found that crystal collectors tend to be drawn to and purchase within a color family during various phases of their lives. They feel comfort and ease when holding a stone of a particular color. This preference often extends to a desire to surround themselves with that color in other areas of their living space and wardrobe. You are likely already aware of your own color preferences, but do you realize that powerful messages from your inner self lie within your choice of colors?

Take a moment to consider the color of clothing that you most often choose to wear. Imagine the color in your mind. This choice can mean much more than simply deciding what to wear each day. The color you choose to wrap around your body holds a deeply personal message to you from your own Inner Guide. Also, the color of crystals you are drawn to work with can help you realize what you need most in life.

I made a wondrous connection in my own crystal work: gemstones of a similar color tended to have a few benefits that were shared across all the crystals of that color. I realized that as I was drawn to working with a particular color of stone, I was genuinely in need of the benefits that color gemstone provided. As I was developing videos for my online content, I discovered the many ways that intuition informs us about what we need – through the crystals and colors we are attracted to. Thus was born the inspiration for this book. I discussed this concept briefly in my first book, *Crystal Wisdom: Unearthing the Power of Gemstones for Positive Life Change*, but I knew even then that I would be expanding this specific topic into its own complete book.

My goal in the Crystal Wisdom series of books is to enable you to access your own inner truth and to use your crystal collection for practical, noticeable benefits. I want to help you choose the very best gemstones to support your life challenges, personal growth, and deep inner healing.

This book will help you discover the ways in which we are influenced by the colors we are surrounded by. It unveils the power in which our intuition provides the information we need through our own color choices. *The Crystal Wisdom of Colors* provides an in-depth explanation of the benefits provided by each color of gemstone. I'll also explain how you can harness the power of crystal colors to cultivate and inspire positive growth in your life.

If you are ready to learn how to decipher and utilize the enlightening messages of crystal colors to improve the quality of your life, then sit back and let's start exploring the exquisite world of color!

PART ONE

Setting the Foundation

CHAPTER 1

DISCOVERING THE WISDOM OF COLORS

Part of the draw of a crystal collection is the beauty of the colors available from the vast array of gemstones. The sparkle, shine, and brilliance that each gemstone displays calls to us to pick it up, hold it in the light, and gaze on this natural delight. This often leads someone attracted to gemstones to buy more and more of them to add to their crystal altars, grids, and display shelves. Color is such a strong magnet when we are buying new crystals. If you have read my previous book, *Crystal Wisdom: Unearthing the Power of Gemstones for Positive Life Change,* then you know that crystals help us tap into a wealth of information about our lives. That attraction to a gemstone or its color can unlock answers you have been seeking. We are born with this source of wisdom, and it accompanies us our entire lives.

The attraction to color is one that starts when we are quite young. Children love to explore and play with color. From paints to clay to crayons, children are not inhibited in expressing their imagination in color. As a child I coveted the packs of crayons with 124 colors! The more color options the better. My son enjoys sets of clay with a wide color variety, and my daughter enjoys massive paint palettes to express her creative visions. Indulging in color exploration comes naturally to children, and this draw to colors does not leave us as we grow older, it just becomes a little more subtle.

Declaring and reveling in a favorite color is a common shared experience when we are children. Choosing a color and delighting in it is a childhood milestone. That color becomes a part of our identity. It is a sacred choice. We would surround ourselves with that color. Our clothes, artwork, school notebooks, toys, bedding, and bedroom walls often included that favorite color. Some children even prefer food only of a certain color.

Children will list their favorite color as an important part of who they are. An introduction to a class of students may sound like, "My name is Kate. I am eight years old. My favorite animal is a cat, and my favorite color is teal green." Yes, kids can be extremely specific about even which shade of color is their favorite. Kids also categorize their friends and relatives by their favorite colors. "Lance and Jenny like blue. Maria's favorite color is pink. And cousin Grace's color is light yellow." It is a subtle discernment between the people in children's lives. Colors help us when we are forming that basic identity of who we are by deciding what things in life we enjoy. It builds up part of the framework for who Kate is.

If you look back in time to those days before adulthood, what was your favorite color? What memories do you have of that color? Childhood favorite colors are often so ingrained in our experience of growing up that we can easily remember all of our favorite colors and what we owned in those colors. We can remember the importance that the color held in how we expressed ourselves to the world, to our family, friends, and classmates. Young adults, in particular, tend to have a specific statement they want to make by wearing and displaying colors in their lives. It becomes one facet of the person and persona we are building as we develop and grow.

As important as colors are to children, the chosen colors are also a transient preference. Children may be totally devoted to a special color one week, then next week it is a completely different color. My daughter just transitioned from a total love of pink to a devotion to sky blue. She no longer wants to wear the pink clothes and is choosing toys in her new color preference. She is not being flighty or indecisive. She is experimenting with how it feels to be surrounded by a light blue world. This process is important to growth and development as children try on new aspects of their personality to see how they feel. My son's favorite color was green for quite a long time and now it is orange. I am continually amazed by their passion for colors. Do you remember other colors you were drawn to as a child? You may also be observing this fluidity of color preference in your own children. This is a natural ebb and flow as young personalities develop and morph. A dance with the various colors to explore how each makes them feel and how they can express themselves.

As adults we become less focused on a specific favorite color. It is not as much a part of our identity, but it does still remain. You may not have consciously chosen purple as your favorite color, but it just happens to take up the majority of your wardrobe. You may choose purple accessories and home décor or buy purple flowers and gemstone jewelry. You continue to surround yourself with a color preference even if it is not declared as part of who you are when introducing yourself to someone new. These colors also ebb and flow over the years. You may notice that you're wearing less purple and more green has entered your closet. The previous couch pillows and curtains have now been replaced with a different color scheme. You reach for a different color of hat or tie when going out. Your color preferences and evolutions of color choice over time can provide you with valuable information.

This book will show you how these preferred colors can tell you more about what you need in life. It will also guide you into a deeper working relationship with the crystals and gemstones you are drawn to. We are attracted to particular colors because they instill a feeling within when we look at or wear the colors. The colors also affect our moods, thoughts, and actions. Whether we know it or not, we are drawn to how a color can make us feel and how it influences us. This is subtle, but every time you buy *another* green hat, *another* green pen, or *another* green gemstone, you are inviting more of the feeling of green into your life. Our own intuition draws us to what we need. The benefit of recognizing this is that we can actually decipher and use the information that color attraction is offering us.

Consider the items in your life right now. What colors surround you? Which colors and shades draw your eye at the store? What gemstone colors do you continue to purchase? This book will provide you with an opportunity to notice and recognize color preference in your life, uncover their messages for you, and notice when color preference changes. A color fondness could be obvious, but you only just recognize it when you stop to look. If it is not apparent, consider what color you would choose for: a shirt, shoes, hat, iPad or phone cover, scarf, towels, sheets, a painting in your office, or a yoga mat. Notice if any recurring color theme arises. This is not an accident. Your Inner Guide is whispering to you. Color preference is an internal yearning to bring more of that color into your daily life, and to cultivate more of the qualities that the color represents.

Identifying this yearning is a powerful step in uncovering vital information that your intuition and inner wisdom are trying to tell you. If you are reading this book, you likely want to know more about the colors you are drawn to, and what your attraction to green, light blue, or white is trying to communicate. You want to access deeper intuitive knowing that can provide you with guidance, support, encouragement, and healing. We know what we need in life, and color preference is a way that our deep inner wisdom offers clues and messages to improve our personal journeys.

Chapter 1: Discovering the Wisdom of Colors

In *Crystal Wisdom*, I discussed how the power of color attraction enables you to choose the best gemstones for your current life challenges. In this book, I will go much deeper so you will be able to discover all the life situations and personality characteristics that a particular color may influence and how you can use it to your advantage. Your fascination with yellow may indicate you need to examine how you feel about abundance and what contributes to and influences abundance in your life. Pink and its domain of love is so broad that it may be challenging to narrow down which area of our heart needs attention. Do we need to give love, love ourselves, forgive or heal our heart? We will explore the various aspects of each color to help you explore, unearth, and cultivate positive life choices, actions, and remedies for your wounds. You'll be able to make your Crystal Wisdom gemstone practices much deeper, meaningful, and effective. You'll learn to surround yourself with the essence and energy of colors that can help you heal and prosper. If you're ready, let's dive into the Crystal Wisdom of Colors!

CHAPTER 2

MY COLOR JOURNEY

As I was on my journey exploring the wisdom offered by gemstones, I noticed that the color of the gemstone had a great influence on the supportive benefits it could provide. Through the process of working with more and more gemstones, I naturally memorized their benefits and could quickly compare one stone to another. This was a great skill for tapping into my own Crystal Wisdom when needed or offering guidance to others. It wasn't long before I started to notice themes arising from gemstones of the same color.

I began to study color as well as the gemstone benefits so I could offer information in a more concise and organized manner. I was fascinated by the role colors played in our emotional, psychological, and spiritual well-being. Using my crystal books, I compared various gemstones in the same color family to see where the benefits overlapped. Color psychology books were a resource I devoured to understand how we react to different colors and the affects colors have on our moods and mindset. In an effort to understand how our energetic body resonated to various colors, I delved into a study of the chakra system. Each chakra resonates deeply with a specific color and working with that color helps bring balanced flow to its chakra point in the energetic body. After compiling all of this information into categories, I undertook the challenge of figuring out how I could combine this knowledge with my crystal practice so as to gain practical use of this wisdom.

I started by examining the colors of my past to reflect on the themes those colors presented. Of course, I was merely gazing back on those colors in my life connecting the moments in my life with color preferences. I could see the colors' themes weave through past life experiences. I used hindsight to identify the signs that I was reaching to the color for support and to recognize the color's influence on my life choices. I offer my revelations to you as an example of how you, too, can explore your past to recognize color's deep influence on your emotional, mental, and spiritual wellness through the course of your life. You will discover the signs that show your Inner Guide was speaking to you and looking out for your Highest Good, trying to steer you toward the path your soul desired and supporting you when you needed to heal.

As a child my color preference changed quickly with the winds. I don't actually remember having a deep dedication toward one particular color. I imagine I was trying them all on to see how each suited me. I do recall having an affinity for bright, primary colors. Primaries are the building blocks for all other colors, and maybe I was relying on those bold colors to shape my own primary base. I remember a particular sweater I loved that was grey with primary color spots all over it. I "borrowed" it from my mother and adopted it as my own. I even wore it for our only family portrait when I was a teenager. All of my formal dresses for school dances were bright and eye-catching. In retrospect, I realize I was trying to stand out and become my own unique, vibrant person during those challenging years of early high school.

The first noticeable color preference occurred after my family briefly lived overseas. We spent a year and a half in Cairo, Egypt, and I was influenced by its warm, earthy colors and relaxed mode of loving. I returned from Egypt wearing light browns and beiges. After a period of trying to be bold and stand out, I settled back into a calmer, more grounded energy. You will explore how the color brown nurtures our desire for growth and a sense of home and belonging when you read Chapter 11. I had returned from a faraway adventure and was rediscovering home. I was leaving behind the immaturity of my tween years and stepping into my transition into a young adult. In this comfort of the grounded energy of brown tones, I was ready to start growing into my future self.

My next color preference arose when I first started college. The color was black. I moved out of my childhood home with my parents in Salem, Oregon, and into a dorm room with other girls in the much bigger city of Portland, Oregon. This was my first time living on my own, with my own responsibilities for my education, safety, and finances. My parents assisted me financially, but I still had to hold a job to fulfill the rest of my financial needs. I was in charge of when I went to sleep, woke up in the morning, how I presented myself when (and if) I went to class, and getting myself to work on time. This was a vast amount of freedom and it felt like the floodgates had opened in my life. I didn't always use this freedom wisely. I wasn't consistent in attendance, stayed up way too late at night, and generally engaged in college mischief.

During this time, I wore black. I mean, I wore head-to-toe black, with black boots and a long black leather trench coat. Wearing black didn't mean that I was depressed, angry, or even up to no good. As you will learn in Chapter 8, the color black has very supportive benefits. This was a time when I needed to feel safe. I wanted to be reassured that outside of the protective arms of my parents, I could still survive. It was quite a vulnerable time for me, and I yearned for security. By wrapping myself in black clothing, and the "armor" of my boots and trench coat, I felt that I could defend myself and survive in this big, wide world.

The phase of black did not last for long. In my early twenties I transitioned to an attraction to green. By this time in life, I had loved and lost, experienced heartbreak, broke some hearts, and suffered from unrequited love. I had been engaged, unengaged, and cheated on. My heart was overwhelmed, and I didn't know how I would manage to have a fulfilling relationship if love was going to be such a challenge. Even as I entered into new relationships, I held a hesitation and an expectation that it wouldn't end well. My mother remembers specifically during this time asking me what color afghan she could crochet for me and was quite surprised when I replied with green. It distinctly stood out to her that this was a change from previous color preferences. In hindsight, it was a very clear message that my heart was aching.

In Chapter 13 you will learn about the heart healing properties of green. My heart needed a soothing balm and reassurance that I would recover from these heart wounds. I surrounded myself in green as I started dating someone new with hopes that this new person would prove that love was worth all the effort. In fact, the man I married during this time also adored the color green. I considered it a sign from the universe that this new person in my life enjoyed the same color. He did indeed contribute to healing my heart during our decade-long marriage. He provided the stable love that I had desired and a healing space in which to recover and strengthen my faith in love.

As I moved past the heart wounds of the past, I began to focus on myself as an adult, and yellow drew my attention. At this stage I was securely employed in a job that was stable and financially rewarding. This job supported me and my husband but didn't inspire any sort of interest or passion within me. I was in the job to be able to pay our bills. I remember telling my friends that I was "still figuring out what

Chapter 2: My Color Journey

I want to be when I grow up." I was also now growing unsatisfied in our marriage, but I wasn't quite sure what to do about that. I was unsatisfied in many areas of my life, but I remained where I was. The leap it would require for me to change my life path would be way too dramatic, and I had no faith that I could succeed. I lacked the confidence and motivation to carve a new future.

Chapter 12 will introduce you to the wisdom of yellow and its messages to examine confidence, motivation, and our mindset about abundance. I needed personal confidence so desperately. My mother was also present during this color transition and was surprised when yellow made its dramatic entrance into my life. I needed to buy a new car. My mom and husband joined me at the car lot for the search and were taken aback when I pulled up in a bright yellow car. I believe my mother's exact words were, "Did Shannon just drive up in a *yellow* car? Really? Yellow?" I had chosen to surround myself with a strong, powerful yellow car. A car that would take me places and compel me forward. This is when I began to take charge of my own direction, started taking certification courses, enrolled in a master's program, and started actively planning a different future.

After my divorce, I immersed myself in my Transpersonal Psychology studies and discovered the insightful and transformative power of yoga. After joining a lunchtime yoga class with a friend, I was completely hooked. More importantly, I was enraptured by the practice of Yin Yoga. This is a style of yoga that invites someone to remain in gentle stretching postures for a lengthy duration. Yin Yoga enables us to explore patience, discomfort, and sitting in a situation that makes us want to flee while remaining in it. The practice of yoga was instrumental in recovering not only from a divorce, but also from discomfort while recuperating from knee surgery. I decided to take yoga teacher training with Jill Sockman of Blue Lotus Yoga in North Carolina. I also enrolled in Phoenix Rising Yoga Therapy training to supplement my exploration of the healing properties of yoga.

The color blue began to creep subtly into my world. It wasn't obvious at first but arose ceremoniously when I graduated from yoga teacher training. Jill presented each graduate with a chakra candle for the chakra she felt they needed to cultivate and strengthen. Each chakra energy center is represented by a color. Jill chose the throat chakra for me and its color is blue. Both the throat chakra and the color blue represent authenticity and personal truth. Chapter 15 will guide you through finding and speaking your truth.

At this time, I was immersing myself in spiritual studies and hiding it from most of my coworkers at my corporate job. I was deeply drawn to the inner world but didn't feel safe enough to share this with a broader audience. I fell in love with the deep blue gemstone Sodalite and kept many pieces around me at home. I would always come back to Sodalite when I felt the divide in me aching. It took many long years of intentional work with the throat chakra to find my own personal truth and the confidence to be open and honest about my authentic self. I will forever be grateful to Jill for her intuitive knowing of my needs and for drawing my attention to it.

Then, as quite the surprise to myself, I fell in love with the color pink. It was a color I had avoided for most of my life because I felt it was just too stereotypical as a "girl's color." I was rejecting the notion that girls had to like pink. One day I was shopping and found myself enjoying and purchasing pink clothing. I was becoming more confident and authentic in my personal decisions, so I decided that I didn't care what anyone else thought about pink, I was wearing it. I was dating again and optimistic about finding someone who was more of a soul match. This time I was much more aware of the type of man I was looking for and was going to rely heavily on my inner wisdom to guide me. My life was ripe for love and true connection. A quirk of fate led me to my current husband, and I knew quite deeply that he was the right person for me.

Pink is the realm of love for yourself and others. As you will explore in Chapter 14, pink helps us examine all the many facets of love and how we may unconsciously be blocking its reception. Pink swept me up in its brilliance and ushered me toward healthy satisfying love. It was a signal letting me know that I was ripe for new loving opportunities, and I am thankful that I was receptive.

Now, at the current point in my personal time line, I find myself embraced by the color of my birthstone, purple. The time came when I knew I could no longer live a professional "double life." Focusing on both a full-time technical job and the part-time spirit work with gemstones was becoming too burdensome. For my emotional sanity and spiritual health, I needed to commit to an authentic career path and give it all my attention. My throat chakra expanded and opened as I retired from my corporate job and dove completely into Reiki Gem Wellness, my gemstone jewelry business and YouTube channel. The focus of my soul drifted upward to my Third Eye chakra, encouraging me to work more with my intuitive nature now that I was no longer distracted by my day job.

Purple is the color of intuition, inner wisdom, and practical wisdom. In Chapter 18, I will discuss how purple enables us to balance all aspects of the space of knowing. This includes "thinking knowing" as well as "inner knowing" and how they can complement each other. My books are created in that purple space touching both my inner wisdom about gemstones and the mind wisdom that helps me craft a message within these pages.

I feel blessed to be able to recognize the signs and messages of color in the present moment. To be able to recognize when my intuition is guiding me with the colors I am drawn to is a gift. It allows me to quickly take a moment to reflect on why the color made an appearance and what the significance is to my day or life path. When orange arises in my life, or when I notice I am working with more orange crystals, I use that as a sign to check in with my creative spirit. It's a sign that I need to incorporate more beauty, movement, and creativity somewhere in my routine. Color wisdom doesn't just reserve its influence for life altering moments. Sometimes the sign can indicate a small but immediate action that would be healthy and satisfying for you. A desire to meditate with or wear my orange gemstones may indicate that the advertisement I saw for the local botanical garden would be a fulfilling activity for my family. Noticing blue before an important meeting could be an indicator to stay true to yourself during the meeting. You can bring a blue gemstone with you to support your communication skills.

Learning the inherent wisdom in colors can lead to an amazing expansion of your Crystal Wisdom practice. It enables you to work with your crystals and gemstones on a deeper level. It is another phenomenal way to connect to your Inner Guide and tap into your inner wisdom so you can live a more intentional and satisfying life.

CHAPTER 3

HOW TO USE THIS BOOK

THIS BOOK IS A COMPANION TO MY PREVIOUS BOOK, *Crystal Wisdom: Unearthing the Power of Gemstones for Positive Life Change*. The practices in this book aren't intended as a replacement for the practices in *Crystal Wisdom*, but to provide you with additional methods and tools to expand your crystal meditation options. Some of the instructions in this book include the same information I offered in *Crystal Wisdom*. If you are familiar with those practices, then feel free to skip over those sections, or to reread them if you'd like a refresher.

Setting the Foundation

As you are reading this book, I recommend that you read Part 1 in its entirety to familiarize yourself with the Crystal Wisdom Color theory, its historical and scientific context, and how to incorporate crystal colors into your current gemstone meditation and practices. This part will provide you with some background into Crystal Wisdom and your own inner wisdom if you haven't yet read the first book. Through the viewpoints of color psychologists, color therapists, and energy workers you'll then learn how we are affected by color. This knowledge provides the foundation for how the colors of crystals can have an impact on our emotions, body, and energetic system. I'll guide you through how to determine if a particular color has a message for you. We will then explore how you can use the wisdom of crystal colors in meditation, Crystal Wisdom practices, and through journaling. By the end of Part 1, you will understand the valuable impact of color and how you can use it to initiate positive life change.

Diving into Color Wisdom

After you have finished Part 1, you can proceed into Part 2 in two ways. If you know which gemstone color you are most attracted to right now, then visit that chapter to discover the Crystal Color Wisdom messages. Identify which benefits of that color you feel you are in need of, find a gemstone of that color to support you, then begin to meditate with it to unveil wisdom, guidance, and solutions to your life goals and challenges. Explore the depth to which this color can influence and improve your life.

If you finish the reflections in Chapter 6 for finding your wisdom color and are not sure which color speaks to you the most right now, you can proceed in one of two ways. If one of the color themes stands out to you, such as transformation, you can head straight to that chapter to see if the supportive benefits of that color are needed to enhance your current life needs. If it's clear to you that you are seeking more love or to connect with your intuition, then discover how incorporating those color gemstones can help you expand that area of your life.

Or, you can choose to read through all the color chapters. Sit with your journal nearby, and take notes about the color qualities you feel you could benefit from. Take note of which color traits inspire the strongest reactions from you. Does a feature really stand out to you, feel really familiar, or trigger you? Those are signs you should explore that aspect in more depth. Note which colors you could benefit from and which gemstones in those color families you are drawn to. You can use this list to purchase gemstones to begin your wisdom practices.

Each color chapter offers four sections of guidance related to that color. The first is in-depth information about a common theme offered by that gemstone color. These themes are subdivided into three more specific attributes of that theme. They are related and represent a different facet of the overall color theme. I offer a list of signs that indicate when you may be in need of the support of that color and symptoms to look for to determine which areas of your life need attention and nurturing. Then, I provide a list of gemstones included in that color family and a description of the additional benefits they provide. Finally, I offer a guided meditation specifically designed to tap into the inner wisdom of that gemstone color.

After you've read through the book however feels natural to you, revisit this as a resource as often as you like. Whenever you notice a color standing out to you, then read that color chapter to uncover the guidance that color is trying to provide you. I often take note of new colors on a daily and weekly basis. This could provide a support message for the day or help guide me through an upcoming week. This book can support your gemstone practices on a regular basis.

The Practice of Journaling

As you ready yourself to begin this color exploration, I recommend the practice of journaling to help put your experiences and feelings into words for future reflection. Take some time to find a special journal that you can dedicate just to this practice. Allow your creative self to guide you toward a journal that speaks to you. If you don't have one already, you can plan a sacred time to purchase one. There is so much variety in colors, styles, and sizes of journals available online. If you'd prefer to see and hold them first, find a local office supply or stationery store for some shopping time. Your connection to your journal will be as strong as your relationship with your crystals and is part of your Crystal Wisdom and Color Wisdom practice.

Once you have your journal, you are ready to begin on the Crystal Color Wisdom journey. This journal will help you from the very beginning as you notice which colors you are drawn to, for recording the messages and insight they offer, and documenting which gemstones you would like to work with.

Why is journaling so important? The act of writing down your inner wisdom will enable you to make its messages concrete. You acknowledge that you received the information from your Inner Guide and are documenting it for further reflection. Journal entries will help you uncover the root source of life challenges, discover patterns of thoughts and behaviors that are causing stress and complications in life, and unveil your authentic life goals and dreams. It is vital to the act of manifesting change in your life.

There is no definitive and correct way to journal. Do not feel limited as to what you should or shouldn't write in your journal. Write down whatever impressions, messages, images, felt sensations, or emotions arise for you. You can draw pictures, write poems, or express wisdom as it is emerging for you. Describe your life challenges and how you felt about them that day. This will be where you start to see how your reaction and feelings about life situations begin to change. As you read over your past journal entries, you will be able to notice progress, perhaps that a particular heartache doesn't feel as intense anymore, or that it's feeling more natural to speak in public, or that you are more patient in frustrating circumstances. The transformation will take shape and come to life the more you practice, and you will be able to witness it within the pages of your journal.

Sending and Receiving Hands

As you proceed into this book, I'd like to clarify some terminology I'll be using throughout the book. One question I often receive is,

"Which hand should hold the stone?" The answer will depend on your intention and how you prefer the energy to flow. When you want to invite in the qualities of the gemstone and its color, you will hold it in your non-dominant hand. This is the hand you do not write with. It is referred to as the receiving hand. If your intention is to send energy out, such as healing energy, love, or forgiveness to someone, then you will hold the crystal in your dominant hand, the hand you write with. This is called the sending hand. If you are ambidextrous, you should designate one hand for receiving, the other for sending, and be consistent with that in practice.

There is also a valuable glossary at the end of the book in which I define the common terminology I use in my Crystal Wisdom teachings. Please refer to this resource if you'd like more context regarding the use of a term or phrase.

Additional Notes

There are a few topics I would like to clarify before we dive into the meat of this book. The first is that there are exceptions to the gemstone color themes. Stones for transformation are not limited solely to grey gemstones. For example, Malachite is known as a powerful crystal to inspire transformation and change, however, it is green, not grey. What I am describing in this book are the traits that all gemstones of a color share. All grey gemstones support transformation, but there are additional transformation gems that are not grey. If you are actively seeking help through a transformation, you can easily explore the realm of grey gemstones first for a supportive crystal. In addition, individual grey gemstones provided even more benefits than transformation. There are so many ways that gemstone benefits can be categorized and presented, however this book focuses solely on the themes by color.

The next clarification is that colors invariably have a global symbolism that differs between countries and cultures. What I will be presenting is the shared benefits that gemstone color represents. This isn't going to match up with every global interpretation of that color; it is limited solely to gemstone color symbolism.

Finally, the chakra system often includes indigo in association with the third eye chakra. Indigo is a color that is hard to distinguish and is often called royal, deep, or navy blue. I will not be including indigo, because I feel those color stones fall more into a classification of either blue or purple based on its supportive benefits. In some references, the color purple, or violet, is associated with the crown chakra, in other references it is white. This book isn't intended to be a chakra gemstone book. While I do use the chakra colors and symbolism to describe what contributes to a colors influence on a person, this book is not meant to correlate gemstones with specific chakras.

CHAPTER 4

HOW DOES CRYSTAL WISDOM WORK?

"The path to wisdom begins with the opening and development of the inner self and on the forms revealed during quiet meditative times."

~ Judith McLeod

What Is Crystal Wisdom?

MY FIRST BOOK, *Crystal Wisdom: Unearthing the Power of Gemstones for Positive Life Change*, describes how Crystal Wisdom works in great detail. It offers ways in which you can identify the gemstones that will be most supportive to your current life challenges (also known as Guardian Gemstones), how to obtain your crystals, and how to design daily and spontaneous practices to enable you to tap into the deep and transformation wisdom of gemstones. I highly recommend that resource to help you form a foundation for incorporating crystal practices into your daily life.

The heart of the Crystal Wisdom practice is knowing that gemstones are used as a key to unlocking access to our own inner wisdom. They act as powerful meditation tools that enable us to look inside and dissolve the barriers blocking our access to our inner truth.

You already know what you want to heal, what you want to improve, and what you want to attract more of in your life. You have this vast amount of wisdom within, and gemstones help to tap into all of that wisdom, allowing you to manifest actual change in your life.

Crystal Wisdom is different than the practice of crystal healing. The field of crystal healing encompasses the act of healing and recovery using gemstones to facilitate the process. Those seeking to ease symptoms of arthritis may look to specific gemstones to ease the pain and reduce its symptoms. This is a vast field that many look to for support and comfort while suffering from physical, emotional, and mental ailments. Crystal Wisdom is a narrower application within this field. It emphasizes a practice of inner reflection and self-discovery to enable us to make intentional and transformational life choices and actions. It facilitates our connection with inner wisdom to find the truth we already hold within.

What Is Inner Wisdom?

When we open up to and start trusting our sense of intuition, we receive the gift of our inner wisdom. The term intuition refers to our sixth sense that provides us with a means of taking in additional information. It is used to describe those gut feelings and the innate knowing that doesn't rely on any proof for us to believe it. It is that sense that maybe something isn't going right, that we should be cautious about something, or that someone we just met isn't trustworthy. Intuition is our ability to interpret experiences from the world around us and have a strong feeling about them without any concrete proof.

You go on a first date with someone and have an uncomfortable feeling while with them. Something informs you that you need to pay attention. Then a friend tells you that this person is known for cheating on partners. Or maybe you are trying to decide if you should take a new job offer but feel unsettled about it. You take a few more days to consider your decision when an even better opportunity arises. Paying attention to our internal reactions to people, situations, and decisions is how we form a sense of intuition. This is how we start to hear our inner wisdom.

We are all blessed with a wealth of information that we don't necessarily access with our thinking brain. There is a core part of oneself that knows exactly what we need in life. It has the solution to our problems, holds the truth about what we need more of in life, knows why we are afraid, and knows how to best take care of us. Unfortunately, many people never open up to this inner voice. Knowing our truth can be a scary journey because we may not feel ready to look at what we have been avoiding. But our inner self, our Inner Guide, loves us and cherishes us.

Your Inner Guide is the voice of your inner wisdom. We can connect with and hear our Inner Guide's messages by strengthening our sense of intuition. It is that part of the essence within you that knows what you need to live the most joyous, satisfying life. Our Inner Guide truly knows what is best for us in life; however, we often don't hear or acknowledge its guidance.

We often erect barriers between our thinking mind and our inner wisdom. Sometimes it's because we don't trust our gut or are afraid to face the answers. At other times, we don't believe our intuition because we just don't have confidence in ourselves or because we are looking for proof first. Maybe we feel we make bad choices and so we can't trust what we know inside. Believe me, looking at the truth may be scary at first, but it holds a vast treasure that can dramatically improve your life. You may not want to think about that bad breakup last year because you're afraid you'll perceive it as all your fault, but your inner wisdom wants to show you what type of relationship you really should be pursuing. Sometimes, to find our way to a better life, we have to look at those dark shadows and see the light that is just beyond them. The practice of receiving inner wisdom is a slow, steady journey of easing down those barriers, trusting ourselves to know what we need, and allowing that voice to be heard.

Hearing Your Inner Wisdom

Our Inner Guide is begging to be heard. It provides us with information even if we aren't listening or seeking inner guidance. Our Inner Guide is not offended that we don't listen to it. This voice is persistent in its desire for us to live our fullest, most satisfying life. It is constantly whispering to us in the form of synchronicities, repeat messages, and in what we are attracted to.

Synchronicities are those times when we find a significant connection between two different events in a short period of time. Have you been thinking of a close friend you haven't seen in a while only to receive a call from them shortly afterward? My mother would often get intense anxiety attacks days, or even hours, before she received a call that a family member was ill or injured. Inner wisdom isn't limited to what our brain knows, but it rises when there is an upcoming opportunity that we should really take seriously.

Repeat signs and messages work the same way. I remember trying to choose between two job opportunities. The benefits and advancement paths were similar and neither seemed to stand out to me in a significant way. Over the course of the next few days, I kept seeing and hearing the name of one of the companies over and over. This was my intuition guiding me in a particular direction. I took that job, and, not only was I really happy with it, that opportunity led to an even better role later on.

Where do you see repeat signs in your life? Do you see the shape of hearts everywhere? Or the same color car more frequently than others? You might explore the deeper meaning of these repeated signs for yourself by journaling on the topic. Each person has a different interpretation of what signs mean to them. We are subconsciously attracted to things that show us the truth and provide the information we need to find direction. If you are attracted to a particular symbol, such as a heart, your Inner Guide may be telling you that some aspect of love is crucial to you at that time. Are you looking for love? Do you feel the need to have more compassion? Do you feel unloved?

We may be attracted to a particular deity, animal, color, music, or gemstone. Looking deeper into why we surround ourselves with an object or energy can tell us vital information about what we should address in our lives. This is precisely how it works with gemstones and we can make this a powerful and intentional practice.

The Wisdom Properties of Gemstones

The historical uses of gemstones have been compiled into countless books over time, including references from many cultures and time periods. This is one reason why there may be many supportive qualities attributed to one stone—different cultures used it in different ways.

Stones have acquired meanings based on what the visual qualities of the stone can represent. For example, the sharp cutting edge of Obsidian has come to signify cutting attachments in one's life. The stripes and patterns on Bumblebee Jasper can represent paths or options available to us. Orbs and eye shapes on a gemstone, like Kambaba Jasper, can symbolize wheels, turning cycles, and timing. The flash and shine of Tiger's Eye and Sunstone represent the sun's bright, shining nature.

As more and more people work with gemstones, they report similar feelings and sensations when they sit with the stone. All of the qualities have been collected and compiled in the many books on crystal healing. The supportive qualities that I describe in this book have come from many different crystal-healing texts. All of my favorite crystal properties books are listed in the References section at the end of the book. I have personally sat in meditation with the gemstones and agree that the properties listed in the books help those areas of my life.

It's important to note that gemstones *represent* these qualities in our lives. They do not magically grant us these abilities. In the Crystal Wisdom practice, you will be using a gemstone to represent a particular aspect of your life. The gemstone acts as a trigger and symbol that will enable you to explore that aspect and relate to it in your life.

Using Gemstones to Hear Inner Wisdom

Now that we have explored how our Inner Guide sends us messages, imagine if you looked for occurrences of synchronicity, repetition, and attraction via gemstones? What if you took the time to listen to your inner wisdom through your love of crystals? This is the heart of the Crystal Wisdom practice. Are you excited to hear the messages from the crystals you are drawn to?

Sitting with gemstones is a practice of self-discovery. The gemstone is the trigger of our intuition, the key, the focus point. The reason we are attracted to certain gemstones, or specific colors, is because our intuition is already guiding us. When we find that we're drawn to a particular gemstone, keep picking it up, and maybe even feel better when we do, it's because our Inner Guide is trying to tell us something.

Gemstone synchronicity is also a meaningful road sign. This happens for me quite often when planning my gemstone YouTube videos. I map out the schedule of Crystal Wisdom videos well in advance, but more often than not, I find myself in genuine need of that particular gemstone during the week I am writing and filming about it. Or, I post a gemstone video describing a benefit that a viewer needs right at that time. It is vital to take note of synchronicities. They are the signs from the universe, the messages from our spirit and angel guides, and the tap on the shoulder from our Inner Guide.

Crystal Wisdom is about allowing us to intentionally open up to this inner knowing. It is about identifying those situations in life that we want support with, finding those gemstones that will support that situation, accessing the related wisdom, and using it to help us make actual change. Crystal Wisdom encourages us to examine why we are attracted to certain gemstones and colors. Can't seem to put Howlite down? Look at the properties that Howlite supports and identify why it keeps speaking to you. Maybe you find that you need the soothing, comforting properties of Howlite because you are experiencing tension and anxiety. You could also be in need of perseverance to get through a major project. Whatever gemstone you are attracted to, take a moment to find out why. It has so much wisdom to offer you.

Sit with Howlite and allow your own inner wisdom to rise up, see the areas in your life that it affects, and how you really feel about it. Does it elicit hesitation, fear, excitement, or enthusiasm? If so, why? Let the wisdom flow. Use gemstones when you need them and discover where you might be blocking your personal development, avoiding things, or not addressing emotions. Or you might be afraid of something, hiding something, or just need to cultivate more of some quality in your life. This is how we develop a relationship with Crystal Wisdom to figure out the truth within.

Actively Channeling Crystal Wisdom to Make Change

The next step in the Crystal Wisdom practice is to take some action in our lives. This is where the actual life transformation happens. Our lives don't get better just from knowing; we also need to make a change, even if it is just a change of attitude. This is where the magic happens.

Maybe you have decided you want to be more patient during frustrating situations. Then sit with a patience gemstone, such as Green Aventurine, whenever you feel impatient. See how impatience feels to you. Where does your body feel it? What does the emotion of it feel like? What thoughts arise? Sitting and watching is the key to hearing the inner wisdom. Consider what made you so frustrated. You might find that you are triggered by a specific personality trait, a situation, or a need for control. What about those situations make you so frustrated? Once you know the trigger and why you may be triggered, you can plan how to address those situations before you are in them. You might bring Green Aventurine with you to a frustrating meeting. Holding it will remind you of the patience you so desire. Sitting with the Green Aventurine helps you to unlock all the wisdom you already know about your impatience. It enables you to learn from it, prepare, and make life changes. It also provides support to you during those experiences.

This is how gemstones can change our lives. Gemstones allow us to live our lives authentically, honestly, and intuitively. Do they make life perfect? No. But they do enable us to navigate the stressors and chaos of life with more intention and mindfulness. They help us make more considered decisions and respond more mindfully to events and relationships in our lives. The practice of Crystal Wisdom ignites alchemy within us. I will show you exactly how to cultivate this alchemy in your own life in the following chapters. You don't have to have any prior experience working with gemstones. We will go through every stage together until you start to see the magic working in your life.

Crystal Wisdom Combined with Color Wisdom

In *Crystal Wisdom,* I briefly discussed how our attraction to color helps us identify gemstones that can support us in daily life. That chapter was merely the tip of the iceberg. Knowledge of colors can enable us to see our lives through an entirely different lens. It can inform us about our motivations, needs, and wounds on a much deeper level. Learning how our Inner Guide speaks to us through our color attraction can deepen your Crystal Wisdom practice and allow you to discover even subtler insights. Learning why you are so attracted to orange gemstones can allow you to dive into how you feel about and experience beauty, movement, and creativity. It can reveal what might be blocking these areas, and how you can expand them and resolve the root cause of challenges and suffering in your life. Combining the extensive information about the effects of colors with your Crystal Wisdom practice will help you choose the very best gemstones to support life challenges and be able to tap into even more wisdom during your meditation practices. In the next chapter you will learn how color works its radiant magic in your mind, heart, body, and energy.

PART TWO

Building Your Crystal
Color Practice

CHAPTER 5

HOW DO CRYSTAL COLORS AFFECT US?

"For when we connect to colour, we connect to what we feel. And when we connect to what we feel, we can start to connect to who we are."

~ Karen Haller

Before we dive into the individual colors, it's important to understand how and why color has an effect on people. This will reinforce the reasons why our Inner Guide naturally tries to communicate with us through colors and why color has a meaning to us when we are drawn to one. The study of color's influence on the human person has a long history. Judith Mcleod states that "image and colour language comes before verbal language." Before there was spoken and written language, stories were documented on stone walls in colorful images. Paleolithic communities developed language from this initial cave art. Color communicated moods, weather, and warnings well before humanity had the words for them. Color taps into this aspect of our primal nature to share similar messages.

In this chapter, we will explore the many areas of color study that focus on health and well-being. Scholars, spiritual communities, and healers have studied the many ways in which color influences our emotions, mind, physical body, and energetic body. These effects have been studied and collected in the fields of color psychology, chromotherapy, the chakra system, and feng shui.

Color Psychology: Color Influence on Emotion and Mind

Much focus has been given to the influence color has on our psychological states. Colors have long been believed to reduce stress, lift moods, increase motivation, improve alertness, stimulate energy, and inspire optimism. The study of color psychology has influenced many professional fields and corporate human resources. These studies formally began in the 1800s and their knowledge influences industries and therapies worldwide.

The first notable study was performed by Johann Wolfgang von Goethe when he published his work, *Theory of Colours,* in 1810. Goethe was an artist fascinated by the way looking at color could impact the viewer. He expanded on Isaac Newton's previous study about how we see color and how color is structured. Not only did Goethe discuss how we perceive color, but he elaborated on its psychological impact on our emotional and mental states. Goethe had this to say about the experience of viewing color, "People experience a great delight in colour, generally. The eye requires it as much as it requires light. We have only to remember the refreshing sensation we experience, if on a cloudy day the sun illumines a single portion of the scene before us and displays its colours. That healing powers were ascribed to coloured gems, may have arisen from the experience of this indefinable pleasure." Goethe felt that colors inspired moods and feelings within us. "The red-yellow gives an impression of warmth and gladness, since it represents the hue of the intense glow of fire, and of the milder radiance of the setting sun. Hence it is agreeable around us, and again, as clothing, in greater or less degrees is cheerful and magnificent." He had a reverence and awe of the world of color and its pervasive influence on the human experience.

Carl Jung also spent much of his career studying how art could inform us about our mental states, interior world, and psychological health. He is known to have said, "Colors express the main psychic functions of man." Jung created a personality typing system in which he divided personalities into four types and then assigned a color to describe the essence of that person. The colors he used were blue (analytical), green (harmonious), yellow (cheerful) and red (exciting). He felt that a person drawn to one of the four colors would have a personality more in line with that color energy. He pioneered art therapy and utilized the mandala as a means to enable his patients to explore their own psychological states, discover personal insights, and bring about mental and emotional healing. Jung dedicated many books to the meaning of symbolism and color in dreams and art, such as *Man and His Symbols* and *The Red Book,* just to name a few. One such example, as written in *Man and His Symbols* is, "the coat is red, which (as has been noted before) is traditionally the symbolic color of feeling and passion."

Another pioneer in color psychology is Angela Wright, who began studying color in the 1970s. Her definition of color psychology is "the effects of the electromagnetic radiation of light on human mood and behaviour—a universal, psychophysical reaction." She mapped personality types and psychological effects to eleven common colors. Wright described red as, "the simplest colour, with no subtlety. It is stimulating and lively, very friendly. At the same time, it can be perceived as demanding and aggressive." She spoke of orange as "a combination of red and yellow, orange is stimulating and reaction to it is a combination of the physical and the emotional. It focuses our minds on issues of physical comfort—food, warmth, shelter, etc.—and sensuality. It is a 'fun' colour." Angela Wright also developed the

Colour Affects System. This system describes four color families that correspond to four primary personality types. Each color family would share psychological traits. Exposure to each of the four color families will elicit an emotional response in the viewer. Being surrounded by your own color family would enhance a feeling of wellness, balance, and support positive personality features. These color groups could then be used to intentionally influence people. In that vein, the Colour Affects System is often used for marketing and therapy.

Professional industries have embraced the concept of color psychology and these principles are actively utilized today. There are three primary areas in which we can see the use of color psychology in action. Colors are very intentionally chosen in interior design, corporate branding, and for emergency vehicles and signage.

The color of walls can have a dramatic effect on the room's occupants. Interior designers carefully select paint colors to induce a state of mind or mood. Red is often used in restaurants to stimulate appetite. A health food store might use green to reinforce the idea of healthy food. Blue is commonly found in hospitals and healthcare offices because it is calming and soothing. In home décor, a yellow room will help you feel awake and lively. Red in the bedroom can inspire passion. Blue walls can help one relax and focus, which is useful for a home office.

Corporations take great care in selecting just the right colors for the company brand. A strong and memorable brand is vital for the growth and success of a business. The symbol and color should stand out, make sense, and inspire a sense of familiarity. An effective brand will be instantly recognizable. Companies use color to inspire an inherent feeling about that product. Blue is a color representing communication and was chosen for Facebook, Twitter, and LinkedIn. As I mentioned before, green inspires a feeling of health and wellness, so it was a great choice for Whole Foods and Sprouts grocery stores.

Coca-Cola chose red to represent the energy and stamina one would feel after drinking the soda. Corporations large and small know the power that color can add to a company's presence and success and that is the result largely of color psychology.

Finally, we see color intentionally used in emergency road signage, clothing, vehicle paints, emergency vehicles (such as fire trucks and ambulances), and streetlights. Colors are chosen that specifically catch the eye of the viewer and inspire quick action. Hunters wear orange vests, and in the construction industry, signs, vests, and hats are orange. This is to ensure that they are visible and seen in a dangerous environment. Road caution signs are yellow so as to cause the viewer to take notice and look around. They warn you of potential danger. Animal crossing signs, crosswalk, and curve in the road signs are all yellow. Red is also a color that grabs the attention and screams, "Pay attention!" Stop signs, stoplights, fire trucks, and ambulance lights are all red. This is a color that connects deeply to danger and survival. When we see red, we are ready to stop and take immediate action.

Without a doubt color has a tremendous impact on our feelings, moods, and state of mind. It is applied so often in our daily lives to invoke a certain feeling or action. It is used in common phrases to describe our moods. We could be "feeling blue," "seeing red," "tickled pink," or "green with envy." Colors and our emotions are deeply connected, and we will be exploring this phenomenon in depth to tap into our own inner knowing and wisdom.

Chromotherapy: Color Influence on the Body

Chromotherapy is the practice of using the visible light spectrum colors to elicit reactions and healing in the body. It is also called color therapy or colorology. It relies on the electromagnetic frequencies of the color to influence our own human electromagnetic energy to bring it back to a nature balance state of health.

To understand chromotherapy, we need to know the basic properties of light and color. Light energy is projected in electromagnetic waves. Color is produced by various wavelengths of light. The wavelength is measured in nanometers. Each color has its own unique wavelength and frequency. The visible light spectrum is between 380 to 700 nanometers. Each object we see absorbs these color waves; however, the color we recognize with our eyes is the color light that is *reflected off the object*. We observe a banana as yellow because it is absorbing all other colors and is reflecting the yellow waves toward our eyes. White is seen when an object reflects all colors, and black occurs when all light is absorbed by the object. These reflected lights are not halted by contact with our eyes or skin. That electromagnetic energy is taken into the body. It is this acceptance of color into the eyes and skin that is the basis to color therapy healing.

Physicists have argued that nothing *is* a particular color. That color is not inherent to the object but merely exists when it is seen. Color is an experience of viewing and interpreting the color in our mind. Therefore, color requires living interaction. Whether we are absorbing the color with our eyes, or with our skin (as with blind people), the color doesn't exist unless there occurs an interaction being energy and beings. This interaction underscores the deep, intrinsic connection between person and color.

In the practice of chromotherapy, color is believed to be absorbed into the body and causes a physical reaction that can lead to a balance or imbalance within the body. An imbalance leads to illness, and that illness can be cured by bringing the body back into balance with other colors.

The body is said to absorb color in a variety of ways. The most common is by shining a colored light on the body to be absorbed through the skin. One could eat a high concentration of a certain color of food. You could gaze upon a colored sheet of paper, wear single-colored clothing, or do meditation visualizations. For the purposes of this book, when we hold or gaze upon a crystal, we absorb the energy of its color.

The belief in and use of color for physical healing is an ancient practice. The Ancient Egyptians relied on the therapeutic application of color in healing. There was a temple in Heliopolis that had at its apex a crystal. The light would shine upon this quartz prism and divide the light into several different colors. These colors were directed into separate rooms, each with its own unique purpose for healing based on that color. The Ebers papyrus, written around 1500 BC, is a lengthy document that prescribed colors to resolve many common ailments.

Formal study of color on human physical health can be traced back to Hippocrates (460–370 BC). He studied the fluids in the body, which he called humours, and associated a color with each of the four humours. Hippocrates labeled these as: black bile, yellow bile, phlegm (green), and blood (red). He believed that an imbalance of these fluids would cause disease and emotional suffering.

Avicenna was a Persian physician, born in 980, who discussed the use of color in healing treatments in his book *The Canon of Medicine*. He described how to diagnose illnesses by analyzing the patient's skin color, and also how to apply specific colors to practical healing.

How much of chromotherapy is theory and how much is fact? Well, we do know that blue light of wavelengths 430–490nm is a proven method to treat neonatal jaundice. This blue light breaks down the excess amount of bilirubin in an infant's blood that leads to jaundice. UVA and UVB light are current treatments for eczema and psoriasis. There are now UV-free treatments that utilize blue and red LEDS lights that are highly effective for these skin ailments as well. And we also know that exposure to natural sunlight helps our bodies make Vitamin D. This Vitamin D is essential for our bodies to absorb and utilize calcium. It keeps our bones strong and prevents osteoporosis. Vitamin D is also vital in relieving the symptoms of depression.

Sunlight contains a perfect balance of all colors. Light has been proven to alleviate symptoms of Seasonal Affective Disorder (SAD). SAD is caused during the fall and winter months when there is less light during the day and that light is diminished by clouds and rain. This leads to major depression and lethargy. When we absorb natural sunlight, we are exposed to a balanced array of colors, which has a healing effect on our moods and mental health. Once spring arrives, the clouds part, natural sunlight shines forth, depression departs, and the person's mood lifts.

There is no consensus on the extent to which color can generate physical healing and cure illnesses. There are some proven light treatments in use today, and it is generally accepted that natural sunlight, in moderation, is a wonderful support for our body to maintain good health and for recovery from illnesses.

Chakras and Feng Shui: Color Influence on Energy

In addition to an effect on our mind, heart, and body, colors are believed to have a therapeutic impact on our energy system. Everything in this universe contains energy of some form. Energy is the inherent force that provides vitality and power. Even rocks, trees, and my favorite coffee mug holds some level of energy. The energy of a person enables us to move, think, grow, reproduce, and heal, among many other activities. Low energy makes us feel tired and unmotivated, while high energy levels cause us to feel active and ready to move. Our energy body, this field of energy within us, has its own system of health beyond the health of our physical body. There are many practices that manipulate and balance the energies of the body, but I will be highlighting two, the chakra system and feng shui, because they also incorporate crystals into their practices.

The chakra system was first documented in Hindu texts as early as 1500 BC. Chakras are energy vortices within the energy body. The word has been translated from the Sanskrit word for "wheel." Both a vortex and a wheel turn and spin. These chakras are located in various locations within the energy body but are mapped to physical locations in our human body. The spinning chakra enables energy to flow smoothly throughout the body. Each chakra has an interior opening that looks much like the eye of a hurricane; it regulates the amount of energy that flows through the chakra point. If all chakras are spinning at an optimal pace, with an open center, then the energy flow throughout our system is balanced. Margarita Alcantara, in her book *Chakra Healing*, compares the energy flow within the body to the circulatory system of blood. Our heart pumps blood throughout our body. An unhealthy heart is not going to transmit blood at an optimum rate and will cause illness. A chakra that is not spinning in a healthy way will prevent a balanced flow of energy through the body and cause observable symptoms.

There are seven primary chakra locations, but there are said to be up to 114 known chakras in the energetic body. Each chakra contributes to the health and well-being of a subset of the emotional, mental, physical, and personality traits of a being. These chakras also resonate deeply with specific colors. If we revisit color wavelength, the energy of a chakra is said to be nurtured and balanced by a certain color wavelength and frequency. When the color is reflected onto our energetic body it is absorbed by and sustains a particular chakra.

ROOT CHAKRA
Black and Deep Red
Survival and Safety

SACRAL CHAKRA
Red and Orange
Creativity and Passion

SOLAR PLEXUS CHAKRA
Yellow and Gold
Personal Power and Self-Esteem

HEART CHAKRA
Green and Pink
Love and Self-Acceptance

THROAT CHAKRA
Light Blue or Blue
Communication and Truth

THIRD EYE CHAKRA
Indigo or Purple
Intuition and Thought

CROWN CHAKRA
Purple, White, or Clear
Spirituality and Enlightenment

A chakra practice aims to identify imbalances of the chakras, and to bring energy back to balance, therefore encouraging health of all levels of our being. One can identify an imbalance through meditation and visualization, examining emotional traits, physical symptoms, and even with tools like pendulums and energy techniques. There are a number of practices to bring a chakra back to optimum flow, such as: crystal work, color exercises, meditation, yoga, essential oils, energy manipulation techniques, mantras, breath work, and many more.

This Crystal Color Wisdom practice is influenced by the chakra system but is not intended to be an exact mapping to the chakras. The primary focus is on the beneficial effects of crystal color on our energy, spirit, heart, and mind.

Feng Shui is another energy practice that is practiced worldwide. The art of feng shui focuses on the balance and flow of ch'i within our bodies and environment. Ch'i is the life force energy and breath that provides vitality and nourishment to everything in this universe. Sarah Rossbach and Lin Yun, in their book *Living Color: Master Lin Yun's Guide to Feng Shui and the Art of Color,* describe ch'i as the "non-biological self—our spirit, our psyche, or essence." Ch'i circulates not only within people, but in plants, mountains, soil, buildings, and everything we interact with.

Lin Yun emphasizes that color has a dramatic effect on everyone from the moment we open our eyes in the morning to deep within the dream or meditation states. We see the color of our home walls, see and consume the color of our foods, wear color most of the day, and see it continually in our environment. He explains, "When these colors come in contact with our eyes our ch'i is affected, causing a chain reaction." This chain reaction of ch'i influences our thoughts, emotions, and actions; therefore, directing the course of our daily lives.

Rossbach and Yun describe a myriad of ways in which the proper balance of color can dramatically improve our health, abundance, and happiness. These include interior and exterior business color themes, clothing, food, transportation, rituals, and meditations. For example, a health-care worker wearing pink, light green, or light blue will feel and exude a feeling of hopefulness. Eating red foods will strengthen the blood and heart. But a red car should be avoided for someone who is excitable, as it might cause them to be more reckless and have an accident. Colors can also be used to influence one's ch'i and modify personality traits.

In summary, our energetic body has an influence on our overall health. Imbalances in energy amount or flow can have consequences on our physical, mental, emotional, and spiritual welfare. There are many practices that can measure energy health and bring it back to balance to encourage healing and growth. Color is an element that can influence the energy flow of our body and modulate our moods, personality traits, and ability to evolve emotionally and spiritually.

CHAPTER 6

FINDING YOUR WISDOM COLORS

THE FIRST STEP IN SEEKING THE COLOR WISDOM within our crystal practice is to identify which colors are prevalent in your present life. These colors hold messages that can enable you to uncover the deep inner knowledge you already possess. A wisdom color may stand out and declare itself boldly, or it may sneak in around the edges. It may not always be easy to determine just which color is guiding you at the moment. Just as we are able to recognize the messages from our Inner Guide, we can use the same guidance to help discover the colors your soul is seeking.

The act of discovering your guiding colors is a marvelous mindfulness exercise. You have the opportunity to look at your life, the objects within it, and daily occurrences in a focused manner. You will get to examine your daily life to see the beauty, wonder, and wisdom around you. Take this opportunity to peel back the wrapping paper of your life to see the gifts within.

I recommend reserving some time in solitude to take a deep look at your life and allow your inner wisdom to arise. Find a quiet place to sit where you can reflect and write in your journal. You may want to have a comforting drink with you, put on soft music, or light a candle. Create an environment that will help you relax and focus on listening to your inner voice. Consider the following methods of discovering what your wisdom colors are. Ask yourself the following questions.

What Is Comforting to You?

Consider which objects in your life give you comfort when you are feeling low, stressed, or adrift. These are called comfort objects. They are most commonly employed in therapy for children, but we do still have comfort objects as we grow into adulthood. What items give you a sense of peace, security, or stability when you use them? Maybe when you are feeling overwhelmed you curl up on your couch with your favorite snuggly blanket and watch some movies. It could be that when you have a headache, you lie down and gently cover your eyes with a special pillow. I have a particular coffee mug that I reach for when I am feeling anxious. I make myself a cup of coffee and sit with my warm brew to feel a sense of ease. The object could be anything: a squishy chair, cozy shawl or scarf, flowers, jewelry, a plushie, or a gemstone, just to name a few. You could very well have more than one comfort object.

Once you've identified your comfort items, notice what color they are. What color is the warm blanket, the coffee mug, or the flowers on your windowsill that give you a sense of peace? It could be that the color of the object is contributing to your comfort and could be a valuable clue to your wisdom colors. Write these objects and colors in your journal.

What Are Your Color Preferences?

When we shop for products, whether it be online or in a store, we often have a color preference if there is a choice available. Consider what color you often choose when making purchases. Take a moment for each of the following items and picture it in your mind. As you

Chapter 6: Finding Your Wisdom Colors

read the name of the item, visualize the item, and notice what color it is in your mind. Try to allow your "thinking mind" to take a back seat and just let the color appear naturally. Some people have difficulty visualizing images in their mind, and that's okay. Maybe your inner wisdom prefers a color splash or the word of the color. However your Inner Guide speaks to you, open up to that message. Then write down the item and color in your journal. What color would you choose when purchasing: a hat, scarf, bedding, towels, shirt, purse, phone cover, shoes, wall décor, rug, vehicle, candle, meditation or yoga equipment, jewelry, furniture, kitchen appliances. As you look over your responses, do any color themes arise?

Your own closet is a great indicator of color preference. Notice which color you wear more often than others. Is your closet full of purple shirts that you wear frequently? Is your shirt drawer full of blue shirts? Keep in mind that we may own clothing that we don't wear often. Your closet could be full of green because that used to be a preferred color, so try to consider clothing you currently choose. Of course, we don't dress in a monochromatic fashion. There will be a mix of colors, but notice which one color contributes to a larger percentage of your wardrobe. This one method works for me to regularly check in with my heart and mood at the beginning of the day. I intentionally own clothing of every color in this book. I try to dress letting my intuition be my guide. Then I sit there for a moment after getting dressed and ask Inner Guide why I may have chosen to wear yellow that day. Is there an area of my life that requires a little more motivation or confidence? How can I support that quality during that day?

Of course, in a gemstone book we should consider the crystals we surround ourselves with. The color of crystal we reach for is a valuable indicator of what we need to pay attention to. What gemstone colors are you often drawn to? When you are near your crystal collection, which gemstones do you pick up and sit with most frequently? When you shop for crystals, which colors attract your attention most often? Write down some of the gemstones you currently feel drawn to.

There are some standouts when it comes to color preference. Occasionally, color choice may stem from something that is unrelated to the color itself. For instance, some people dress to complement their hair or skin color. If this is the case, do you also choose these colors beyond the scope of your wardrobe? You may decide to wear one color because it looks good on you, but then choose to surround yourself with a different color entirely. Whatever lies beyond the intention of complementing your hair, skin, and eyes is your true color preference. It may indeed be the same color.

Some others choose colors based on a sports team, school, city, or country. I know many people that buy in a certain color palette because those are the colors of their favorite team. This situation could still hold some inner wisdom. Consider if you chose the team because it is a local team or because you liked the colors. My mother chose her favorite football team because she liked the colors. If it was a color choice, then that is a valuable hint. Then think about when you wear those colors. Do you only wear the colors to represent the team, or do you still tend to surround yourself with the colors even when you're not displaying team pride? If so, write down those colors.

What Colors Are Repeatedly Arising?

This reflection may take a little more time to uncover. As you are sitting in your comfortable space with your journal, notice if any colors have been showing up in your daily routine over and over. Maybe you tend to notice yellow buildings, cars, and flowers more often than other colors. Sometimes the color can appear in song lyrics, mentioned in books you are reading, or in tarot and oracle card readings. Does a color seem to be following you around?

Chapter 6: Finding Your Wisdom Colors

Repetition is a powerful method of seeing the signs and "hearing" the messages from the universe, spirit guides, or from whichever beings we consider sacred or divine. Many people notice heart shapes wherever they go. They see it in the shapes of shrubbery, flaws in the sidewalk concrete, in the swirl of beach sand, or the shape of a rock. There are social media accounts entirely dedicated to the synchronicity of hearts in the account holder's life. Angel numbers are another example of the power of repetition. People look for repeating patterns of number such as 222, 4444, 1234 and so on. People might notice them on store receipts, money, house numbers, clocks, and anywhere that displays numbers. Seeing a particular angel number pattern over and over has its own unique angel message.

It might not be apparent as you look back on your days, but now that you've considered color repetition, pay attention over the next week to what colors pop up throughout your days. You may want to keep a little notebook with you to write down when these occurrences happen. Color repetition could arise in plants, animals, artwork, book covers, buildings, signs, cars, objects that fall in front of you, the Internet, lyrics, text, packages, other people's clothing color, and much more. Over the course of a week, do any colors stand out?

I remember a particular week in which I kept dropping objects that were pink. I spilled a box of pink business cards, tripped over a pink box, dropped and broke a pink mug, and knocked over a lit pink candle, spilling pink wax all over. It was irritating that I was being so accident prone until it occurred to me that the accidents had something in common. I sat with a pink gemstone in meditation and asked it gently to tell me more. What arose was a message that I was irritated with a family member and my heart was feeling strain. I needed to have a talk with this person and discuss this frustration. After our talk, we both felt seen, heard, and understood. Our relationship had been brought back to a place of harmony and peace.

That was the message being shown to me from my Inner Guide using the color pink.

Where Are Synchronicities with Color Occurring?

There is one more way in which your Inner Guide could be providing a message for you. As I briefly discussed in Chapter 4, synchronicity could provide some valuable guidance. Synchronicity is when two things occur simultaneously and seem significant to each other, but don't have a discernable connection to each other. One event didn't cause or influence the other event, they just occurred closely in time with one another. These are coincidences that seem very meaningful.

An example of synchronicity is when you are thinking of a friend and they happen to call right at that time. You are humming a song and then hear it playing somewhere right after. You are choosing between two jobs and you see signs of one of them appear throughout your day. For my last birthday, my mother got me a brand-new set of knives. I had actually been shopping for knives, but I hadn't told her at all. I had told no one, in fact. She didn't have access to my Internet searches for knives. But when I unwrapped her gift, it was a fabulous new set, just what I needed. Many of my clients have purchased a particular gemstone, and then I post a video for that gemstone the very next day. I get reports of that synchronicity on a weekly basis.

It may take some time to notice synchronicity with colors. This is when a life situation or challenge occurs in time with a color. For example, you could be experiencing difficulty working on a creative project. Whenever the project comes up in your life you also notice the color orange. You're trying to start on that painting, and you happen to be eating oranges. You may be trying to generate ideas, and your attention keeps getting drawn to the orange flowers on a book nearby. Your Inner Guide is directing you toward the color orange to indicate that you should sit with the color orange and specifically reflect on your project. Maybe whenever you see that ex that you are convinced you are completely over, you notice the color green. The person is wearing green, surrounded by green plants, or you're holding a green cup. This could mean that you still need some heart healing when it comes to that past love. That you've been denying the hurt they caused, haven't allowed yourself to process and release it, or that you really still miss them.

Like repetition, this method may take observation over a length of time to notice its occurrences. Stay alert and open to the possibilities. Don't ignore coincidences. Write them all down. Over time you will see the signs and messages from your Inner Guide.

What Colors Do You Choose for Artwork?

Here is another exercise to help you determine which color may be offering you wisdom. You will need some white paper and some coloring supplies. Crayons, colored pencils, markers, or paints are possible options. Sit at a table during a quiet time and arrange the colors of your chosen medium in front of you. Close your eyes, bring your attention to your breathing, and allow your mind to settle a bit. Open your eyes, choose a color, and start drawing. It doesn't matter what you draw, but allow your hands and the color to flow on the paper. If you have various shades of that color, you might want to add the extra shade. If you are called to a second color, you can add that, but limit this to two colors at most.

When you feel finished, take a moment to look at and absorb the color and imagery on your paper. Is it all one family of colors? If it is more than one color, which color takes up more space on the page? Then you can go to those color chapters in this book and read more about why you may have chosen those one or two colors. This is a very simple way to do a quick color reading to guide your day or week.

You can also perform this exercise with gemstones. This requires a set of gemstones including all thirteen colors in this book. Spread them out in front of you. Close your eyes, bring your attention to your breathing, and allow your mind to settle a bit. Open your eyes and pick up the first stone that draws your attention. Sit with it for a few minutes, holding it in your receiving hand. Allow the gemstone energy to settle into your own energy field. Then refer to that color chapter in this book to learn more about that color's messages.

These are just a few methods to determine guiding colors. Not all may bear fruit. One method may speak to you much more than others. Buying preference tends to be a loudspeaker for many. Some exercises are quicker than others, so are helpful for more immediate guidance. These are a selection of methods you can explore to see which colors speak to you the most. Take a look at your journal and see if any one or two colors show up with more frequency. Your list may include many colors, but see if any stand out to you.

What do you do if no color particularly stood out to you? I recommend reading through the color chapters and see if you find yourself in need of a particular quality described in the chapters. As you read, take notes in your journal about the supportive benefits that you are drawn to and are relevant to your life right now. Then you can intentionally work with that color to uncover more insight and find resolutions to that life need.

Once you've identified a color or two, I'll show you how you can use this information to support practical life situations, how to choose the best gemstones to include in your Crystal Wisdom practices, and the way to tap into deep inner wisdom using the guidance of color.

CHAPTER 7

ADDING COLOR TO YOUR CRYSTAL WISDOM PRACTICE

Now that you've identified a color, or even a few, I'll guide you through some of the ways you can start working with it to initiate positive life change. First, I describe how you can find the best color gemstones for your life situations, how to sit with them in meditation to unlock inner wisdom, and how to incorporate these practices into your Crystal Wisdom practice.

Choosing Your Guardian Gemstones

Guardian Gemstones are those gems that will support you during identified, current life situations. A Guardian Gemstone set consists of three to six gems that should be located with easy access when you need their support and guidance. This set of crystals will become your team of guides, protectors, and a source of comfort during your process of inner exploration, daily meditations, and navigation of life's challenges. The guardians will be there for you whenever you need help. I describe the step-by-step process of selecting Guardian Gemstones in the book *Crystal Wisdom*. You can form your Guardian Gemstone set by identifying which life situations you want support with, noticing your attraction to certain gemstones or colors, or by utilizing the guidance of your birthdate. In this book I expand on how you can best select guardians by examining color preference and occurrences in your life.

Use your color discoveries from the previous chapter to help you select just the right crystal to aid you right now during everyday life situations. Begin by reading the chapter(s) related to the color(s) you selected. Take note of any of the crystal color benefits that are relevant to current life needs. Try to be as specific as possible when you are describing the situation. You'll want to be able to bring the issue to your heart, mind, and body during meditations to seek more guidance. You'll need to be able to recognize the situation when it occurs so you can use your crystals when needed. These life needs could include situations that are causing you suffering, qualities in your life that you want to cultivate and expand, decisions that you are having difficulty making, or emotional wounds that you would like to heal.

Once you have chosen a color theme you would like to cultivate, and have identified your life needs, then you can move right to the pages listing gemstones of that color. Read through the list of gemstones with your journal nearby. You will be choosing a crystal to represent that scenario and to inspire transformation. Although all crystals of the same color inspire the same collection of supportive qualities, each stone also offers additional, unique benefits. See which descriptions call to you, feel familiar, and can offer some other support you may need. Look up pictures of the gemstones on the internet or in gemstone books to see which ones draw your eye. Once you have chosen a stone, make sure you have one available to sit with. It may be a gemstone that is already in your collection, but if not, then you'll need to buy a piece.

Sitting with Your Crystal Color

It is important to sit and meditate with your gemstone on a regular basis. In *Crystal Wisdom*, I describe daily and spontaneous practices in great detail as the primary tools for tapping into inner wisdom and initiating transformation. I will describe those practices briefly later in this chapter, as well as offer a new meditation for sitting with the energy of the color for guidance and insight. We can only cultivate change in our lives if we give the situation regular focus and take action. This is accomplished through regular meditation, journaling, and using your gemstones when your life situation arises.

Creating Your Meditation Space

A vital Crystal Wisdom tool is a regular space to sit and perform your meditation practices. This helps to cultivate a regular routine and to help you settle quickly into the Crystal Wisdom reflection process. This is a space that you will carve out from the rest of your daily life and reserve for sitting in quiet. The more often you meditate, the stronger and more familiar your meditation space's energy will become, and you'll be able to settle into your inner wisdom space quickly.

Your meditations should occur in a quiet space in your home that won't be getting much traffic from the rest of your household members. You want to be able to sit and focus on your internal experience, the feeling of the gemstone energy, and how you feel about the life situation you are addressing with the crystal. It is difficult to do this with lots of noise and distractions. You do not need to set aside an entire room for your practice, just a small space in a room where you can close the door and have some solitude.

You'll need a seat for your sessions. This could be a meditation cushion (often called a zafu or zabuton) on the floor. If sitting cross-legged on a cushion is uncomfortable, you can also sit in a chair. Whichever chair you select should be comfortable but not so soft that you drift off to sleep. This chair should be reserved just for this practice. Pulling in a dinner chair every day for your practice will disrupt the energy of the space and be an extra bit of work you need to do before practice, therefore, making the process a little cumbersome. You want to be able to have a regular, set space that you can sit in at a moment's notice.

You may also want to set up relaxing and spiritual objects in your meditation space. Having a small table nearby to place a candle, incense, journal, bell, gemstones, or any critical spiritual items will mark this space as sacred. Setting the scene like this, and creating a designated meditation space, will encourage and reinforce your practice and enable you to tap into the gemstone energy and your inner wisdom easily and quickly. This intentional space marks your practice as special, sacred, and devoted to your own personal growth and development.

There will be times when you perform your spontaneous practices wherever you happen to be, which is entirely acceptable. I encourage you to bring your practices into your daily life. It expands your reflection and healing process out from one small meditation space to incorporating it wherever you are. Most of my gemstone sessions happen right in the middle of the bustle of life. If I feel scattered and disorganized while working, I'll sit in my workspace with some Fluorite to help me focus and organize my thoughts. If I need some patience while teaching my kids, I will sit with Howlite right there in the learning room and invite patience in with us. If I recognize the life situation I have chosen, I often just get my stone, sit down right where I am, and reflect on how that situation makes me feel and how I can best address it. This is how you truly start initiating transformation and change in your life.

Learning the Meditation Posture

For your daily practice, you'll want to sit in a comfortable position that will allow you to be alert and pay attention to the wisdom rising within. Proper posture will allow you to focus less on any physical discomforts and more on how your body, heart, and mind are reacting to your life situation. It's hard to notice the soft, subtle voice of your inner wisdom when you're sitting position is causing your back to ache.

Whether you're on a cushion or a chair, sit up straight but not stiff like a toy soldier. Imagine a string is running from your tailbone, up your spine, and out the top of your head. Then you gently pull the string up and straighten yourself. There should be some looseness but not hunching over. Bring your shoulders back just a touch. This will help open up the heart space and allow you to breathe easier. Tuck your chin down so your gaze rests on the floor in front of you rather than straight ahead. This also allows for greater airflow into your lungs. Check that your tongue is relaxed in your mouth and not stuck to the roof of your mouth.

You should be able to inhale through your nose and out your mouth easily. You can rest your hands lightly on your lap, palms up or down. I recommend putting your palms down if you feel you need centering and grounding. Palms up is excellent if you want more energy or to be more alert. You will have a gemstone in one hand but your closed hand with this gem can still be positioned either up or down. In this position, you should be able to breathe fully and efficiently. Your energy will be able to flow unimpeded throughout your body.

If you have chosen to sit on a cushion, make sure that your sitting bones are evenly planted on the cushion so that you're not leaning right or left but solidly in the center. This provides secure grounding and connection to the earth during this practice. If your hips or knees tend to ache after a few minutes, you may want to have additional supports available to place under your outer thighs to alleviate the pressure. These could be small pillows or even folded towels.

For sitting in a chair, make sure that you can place the soles of your feet flat against the floor. This firm contact to the ground is your source of grounding and centering during this practice. Crossed legs or ankles will not allow the energy to flow evenly and openly through your body.

If you are not used to sitting in meditation, it may take a few weeks to get accustomed to this posture. That is completely normal. Be gentle with yourself and your process of learning. It will start to feel more natural the more you practice. It is okay to move and adjust your position during your meditations. You are not required to be an unmoving statue.

Sitting with Your Gemstones

Now that you know how to sit, there is some guidance that is specific to meditating with gemstones. It is recommended that when sitting for daily practice, you make skin contact with the stone. This helps to strengthen your connection to the stone and its energy. You will be able to feel its surface texture, the weight in your hand, and feel it warm to your touch. However, if you are working with a gemstone in a pendant and the frame prevents you from making strong contact with the stone that is perfectly fine. The practice will still work. If you happen to drop your gemstone on the floor, then pick it up and touch it to the crown of your head. This is an act of honoring and showing respect and reverence for your sacred tools.

Consistent Journaling

I have mentioned writing in your journal many times already in this book and I can't stress its importance enough. Through the practice of journaling, you will bring clarity and definition to your feelings and experiences. It will enable you to recognize themes occurring in your life. You will be able to read back through your entries to notice evolution and change taking place as a result of your reflection and

Crystal Color Wisdom activities. Make sure you are taking the time to write after your meditations, to jot down signs and synchronicities you notice, and to reread your writings regularly. Sometimes it may seem that the work you've been doing isn't yielding any results and you may feel discouraged. This is an appropriate time to read through your entries so you can realize and recognize that change is happening.

Sit with Your Color to Uncover Its Wisdom

Whenever you feel the desire to explore a color occurrence or attraction in your life, you can try this guided meditation. Set aside approximately twenty minutes for this practice—ten minutes to reflect with your gemstone and ten minutes to journal. Before you begin, choose a gemstone of the color you'd like to reflect upon.

I recommend having a routine or ritual to set up or begin your practice. This could be lighting incense or a candle, ringing a bell, saying a short prayer to your angels or spirit guides, or chanting some mantras. This is something to signal the beginning of your practice.

- Pick up the stone and place it in the receiving hand.
- Close your eyes and focus on the feeling of breathing. This will draw your attention away from external concerns and into your body where you will tap into the Crystal and Color Wisdom. Just breathe for about a minute or ten slow breaths.
- Bring your attention to the gemstone in your hand. Notice how it feels in your hand, the weight, the shape, and the texture.

- Imagine the color in your mind or open your eyes and gaze on the color of the stone—whichever feels most comfortable to you.
- Notice any emotions, physical sensations, thoughts, or images that arise when you focus on the color.
- Ask your Inner Guide, "Please tell me more about what (insert color) would like to tell me." Allow a few minutes for this wisdom to arise.
- Ask your Inner Guide, "What is important for me to realize about this life need?" Allow a few minutes for this wisdom to arise.
- Ask your Inner Guide, "What can I do to improve this situation?" Allow a few minutes for this wisdom to arise. Do not be discouraged if the message is hard to notice at first—it will get clearer with practice.
- Thank your Inner Guide and your gemstone for its guidance and then take a few more slow, deep breaths.
- When you feel ready, open your eyes.
- Take a few minutes to write down what you experienced during the meditation, and the wisdom you received.

Daily and Spontaneous Practices

This color meditation is one that you can add to a regular routine of Crystal Wisdom daily and spontaneous practices. The daily practice is the primary tool for tapping into your inner wisdom to uncover more depth and insight into your life needs. During the daily practice you would sit with a Guardian Gemstone and its associated life situation to invite new insight, wisdom, and resolutions to arise. The daily practice allows opportunities to rotate through a selection of gemstones, one per day. You use this information to help you discover ways to heal, resolve, or expand aspects of your life that will lead to a happier, more satisfying life.

If you're noticing a color theme appearing in your life, you may want to substitute your daily practice for the color meditation described in that color's chapter. This is another valuable way to tap into wisdom. Sometimes it is beneficial to look at a situation from a different angle so as to be able to glean insight by approaching the issue differently. Knowing the supportive benefits of the crystal colors, and sitting with them to connect to your Inner Guide, helps to deepen and strengthen your intuition.

The spontaneous practice is intended to assist you in maneuvering the challenges that arise during your day. When you encounter one of your designated life situations, and feel you need assistance, pick up its Guardian Gemstone to activate its supportive energy. The spontaneous practice enables you to release feelings that cause suffering, boost attributes that can help you, and generally helps in finding peace, calm, and stability when you need it. These practices are the means by which change starts to manifest in your life.

PART THREE

The Wisdom of the
Color Families

BLACK | PROTECTION

CHAPTER 8

BLACK GEMSTONES | PROTECTION

THE COLOR BLACK has accumulated a fair amount of baggage in Western culture. It tends to be associated with the more negative elements in life. It's the designation for evil, the dark side, the shadow self, black magic, the black hat, death, and the underworld. Those looking to appear mysterious or wicked tend to surround themselves in black.

Today, I'm going to ask you to set any preconceived notions of the color black to the side. Whoosh, it's gone! In the crystal-healing world, you want to have black gemstones in your corner. Black gems are incredibly powerful, and this color keeps us safe.

The color black is connected to the energy of the feet and root chakras and the associated element, Earth. These chakras are linked to our basic sense of survival, safety, and will to live. It is exactly this theme that embodies the energy of black in crystal healing and the primary benefits of black gemstones. Those who are attracted to black tend to be seeking grounding, protection, and comfort.

Black Gemstones Help You Cultivate More . . .

Grounding

The color black influences the energy of the feet and root chakras. The foot chakras connect us directly to the Earth. It is this basic connection that gives us a strong sense of grounding.

But what is grounding? Grounding is the feeling of complete, mindful presence in your body, right now. It brings your attention to the present moment. When you are grounded you are aware of what is going on in your body, in your heart, in your mind, and around you. It is this awareness that provides a sense of stability, security, and pure existence. You feel secure and connected to the Earth, like deep roots under a tree. The fluctuating nature of life doesn't disturb you or knock you off-balance.

The root chakra regulates our sense of safety and survival. When you are grounded and aware, you can be responsive to threats to your survival. You know which environments are unhealthy for you, when you need to eat, sleep, and how to cope with stress. Threats can be dealt with in a calm, focused manner.

Grounding also helps us absorb and channel the energy from the Earth. This energy will flow deeper into the root chakra to support the color red. Energy from the earth helps to keep us alive and connected to our existence. However, this connection is a two-way channel. If you are experiencing deep anxiety, stress, fear, or psychic overwhelm, you are experiencing an excess of energy. Through the contact of the foot chakras to the ground, you can send excess and negative energy back into the ground and bring yourself back to a calm, focused balance.

Grounding helps us monitor and moderate our physical health, emotional well-being, and energetic balance. You can determine what you need more of, less of, and how to adjust it until you feel stable. When grounded, you feel whole and centered. You may not feel like everything is perfect, but you can identify what is specifically causing distress or unease.

When holding a black gemstone, you can more easily find your footing, draw in the energy of the Earth, and release excess energy back into the ground. These gems help bring your focus back into your body, clear your mind, and allow you to observe your environment. They will help you find ease, balance, and stability during the chaos of life. In a nutshell, the black stone helps you be here, right now.

Protection

Black gemstones take their energy from the deep secure support of the Earth. Imagine the dark depths of the Earth, down in a dark, cool cave, or the darkness of the womb. In *Paradise Lost*, Milton described black as "the womb of nature." This imagery reflects the dark, solid, and secure energy of Earth protection.

Black gemstones will also wrap you in a shield of protective energy. They help you create safe spaces when you feel overwhelmed and threatened. This is especially supportive if you live or work in a toxic, or hostile, environment. Place black gemstones around your bedroom, or desk at work, to shield yourself from the negative energies and intentions of those around you. While you will still hear what's going on around you, the negative emotions and energy will not affect you.

Without energetic protection, the hostile energies of others can invade your own energy, accumulate around it, affect your emotions, and leave you feeling drained and moody. Deep attachments may even follow you home and prevent you from getting rest. Black gemstones help you to shed all of these attachments and allow you to change locations without taking any of it with you.

The color black supports identifying and enforcing personal boundaries. If you are feeling overwhelmed by the demands and expectations of others, black gemstones help you say, "No." They help you release the need to please everyone, or accept every request for assistance that can leave you feeling overworked and tired.

Too much accumulated negative energy, and lack of healthy

boundaries, can lead people to get sick. Personal safety and survival depend on you being strong and healthy. Survival depends on you getting enough sleep, the right nutrition, and maintaining clean and balanced energy. Black gemstones will help you maintain and protect your physical, mental, and energetic health.

Comfort

Within this "womb of nature" we can feel deep support and comfort. Black is often worn as a color of mourning. This is appropriate as it provides support and protection during the grieving process. We can wrap ourselves in the safe, present energy of black to process our pain and loss. All light is absorbed into black, where it is embraced, hidden and protected.

Black gemstones support us when we are suffering from great loss. In particular, Apache Tears and Smoky Quartz are especially comforting during the grieving process. Holding a black gemstone enables you to create a safe, healing space so you won't be overwhelmed by your emotions. When the pain of loss feels too much, sit with a black gemstone and allow it to envelop you like a weighted blanket, easing your heart and reminding you that you will not break apart from the pain.

The safe space of black is supportive when depression, stress, or anxiety strikes, and during "dark nights of the soul." It is the safe cave in which we can hibernate and rejuvenate. It stabilizes us when we feel we can be bowled over by the difficulties in life. It is only when we are in the midst of darkness that we can see the light emerge and recognize the rays of hope. This color helps you find your footing again when all feels lost.

When you feel in need of deep comfort, sit with a black gemstone to absorb the energy of stability and security. Holding a black gemstone will allow you to "just be," without the need to do anything or take action. It brings you to the present moment and away from the chaos and stressors in your life. You can just breathe, find the stability of the Earth, and release excess emotions and energies down into the safety of the Earth. In this safe space, you can recuperate, process, and heal.

Signs You Need More BLACK Gemstone Energy

Try to incorporate black gemstones into your daily crystal healing practice if you are experiencing the following symptoms or occurrences in your life.

- Regular or prolonged periods of feeling scattered, spacey or disconnected
- Lack of awareness of your physical body
- Frequently feeling scared, anxious, unsafe, stressed or overwhelmed
- Living or working in a toxic environment
- Lack of trust in yourself or others
- Frequent illness
- Feeling hopeless or depressed
- Unstable family life, work, or finances (can cause feelings of fear for survival)
- Chronic pain
- Phobias
- Destructive behavior

BLACK GEMSTONES FOR PROTECTION

These black stones provide grounding and protection, but also the unique supportive benefits listed below. Study these additional healing properties to help you identify the most appropriate stone to assist you.

Apache Tears – Stone of Recovery: The Apache Tear is a more translucent form of Obsidian and shares most of the qualities. This stone is much gentler and slower working than Obsidian. It is extremely useful if you are working through really deep traumas and need to take it slowly. It helps to work with grief, forgiveness, and letting go of the past.

Black Kyanite – Stone of Stability: This is one stone that never needs clearing or cleansing! It will not accumulate negative energies. It aligns all chakras immediately and balances the energies of mind, body, heart, and spirit. It supports deep and steady meditation. This fan-shaped crystal keeps you grounded and focused when reaching out to the spiritual realm. Helps to manifest spiritual ideas into the physical world.

Black Tourmaline – Stone of Protection: It transmutes all surrounding negative energy into positive uplifting light. This crystal lifts your sense of well-being and enables you to feel whole, centered, and balanced. This is a potent crystal to use for home protection. Grid Black Tourmaline around your home for energetic protection.

Hematite – Stone of the Mind: It helps you focus a scattered and distracted mind. Hematite can be used for mental attunement, memory enhancement, original thinking, and technical knowledge. It helps you realize that the only limits you have are the ones you put on yourself—the sky is the limit. Hematite helps you choose just the right words for an effective message.

Jet – The Guardian Stone: This is actually a form of petrified wood, so it feels much lighter than a stone. Jet draws out negativity and helps to release unreasonable fears. This stone guards against violence and illness. It also protects a person or home from unwanted spirit presence.

Nuummite – The Magician's Stone: Nuummite is an ancient stone that can open, activate, and clear all of the chakras. Any energy blockages down the central channel will be dissolved. This stone helps to rid you of attachments and realize when someone is trying to manipulate you. Nuummite is also effective during karmic work. It helps you not to repeat old behaviors, to resolve karmic debt, and to regain energy from the drain of karmic attachments.

Obsidian – Stone of Protection: It exposes the truth and tears down barriers. It works quickly and powerfully, so should be used with care and guidance. This gemstone does not allow you to hide from issues, behaviors, or people that have been holding you back. You see straight to those hidden issues and the root of the problem. In conjunction, Obsidian is very useful for cutting ties, or cords, to unhealthy attachments.

Onyx – Stone of Attunement: Onyx is used to absorb what you need from the universe. It is used to cleanse and sharpen the intuition, so you can better receive this higher guidance. It supports you during mourning and times of deep emotional stress. This stone holds a memory of what has happened to the wearer, which helps with past-life work.

Shungite – Stone of Clearing: This stone is one of the oldest stones on the planet. Shungite is said to protect from all electronic and environmental pollutants. It helps you to release any past life or energetic blockages that are preventing you from progressing on your spiritual path. This stone transmutes stress into a powerful motivator.

Smoky Quartz – Stone of Release: It brings calm and centering, lifts depression, enhances practicality, and generally removes negative energies and brings happiness. This gemstone helps you to release that which is no longer supporting you. It is one of the gentlest grounding stones if you need a softer energy.

Snowflake Obsidian – Stone of Surrender: This stone is very soothing and protects you as you surrender resistance and rest in the support of the divine. It helps you recognize patterns of thinking and behavior that are holding you back and allows you to release them. This teaches you to view mistakes as lessons and to learn from your experiences.

GEMSTONE MEDITATION FOR PROTECTION

This is a guided meditation designed specifically to work with evoking the protective qualities of black gemstones. If you feel in need of grounding, safety, energy clearing, energy release, or stress reduction, then identify a black gemstone and try this crystal meditation. Go at your own pace as you feel comfortable. The more familiar you are with the energy of your gemstone, then the less time you may need to meditate to attain the benefits.

Chapter 8: BLACK GEMSTONES | PROTECTION

1. First, locate a black gemstone to use during this meditation.
2. Find a comfortable place to stand. For this meditation you will need your feet in direct contact with the ground. Your foot chakras will be activated and directing energy. It can be inside or outside, as long as you can stand comfortably for about ten to twenty minutes.
3. Hold the black gemstone in your nondominant hand. This is your receiving hand that will take in the energy of the crystal.
4. Close your eyes and begin to take slow deep breaths.
5. Bring your awareness to where your feet are touching the ground. Take a moment to feel the floor or ground underneath you. You are completely supported and protected by the entire Earth underneath your feet.
6. Bring your attention to your body and take note of how your body, mind, emotions, and energy feel right now. Don't try to fix, change, or judge any experience, just take note. Be IN your body and see how it feels.
7. Now take a minute to feel the stone in your hand. Take note of its weight, smoothness, texture, and how it feels as you hold it.
8. Imagine a bright bubble of energy forming around you. It may be difficult at first to hold this visual, but it will get easier with practice. You will eventually be able to hold the image of the bubble around entire rooms, cars, and

homes. This bubble is a solid, energetic barrier and will protect you from any outside influences.

9. Then imagine the chakras in your feet opening up to receive energy from the Earth. Receive this energy and let it flow all throughout your body. It strengthens your energy, aura, and the protective bubble around you. If you feel overwhelmed, allow any excess energy to flow right back down into the ground forming strong energetic roots connecting you to the core of the Earth.

10. This Earth energy is dissolving and detaching any negative energy connected to you and your aura.

11. Allow this loose negative energy to flow right down into the Earth like a thick, dark smog, where it will be absorbed and cleansed.

12. Imagine yourself now, completely protected, cleansed and present in the moment. Sit with this visualization as long as you feel comfortable.

13. After a few minutes, bring your awareness back to your breath and body. How does your body, mind, emotions, or energy feel now? Has anything changed since the beginning of the meditation? Don't try to force anything. It may take several meditation sessions to notice real change but take note of anything.

14. Then release the imagery and come back to your breath. Just breathe and feel the Earth underneath your feet.

15. Take a few final deep breaths.

When you feel ready, open your eyes.

Take a few minutes to journal about your experience.

RED | ENERGY

CHAPTER 9

RED GEMSTONES | ENERGY

At 620 nanometers, red is the color of light that penetrates deepest into the skin. It is the most vital to our ability to function and survive. Red penetrates deeply and forms the foundation of our experience on this Earth. Holding red gemstones will have a dramatic and fundamental effect on our daily experience.

Red is the color of life force energy. It is the color of blood, love, and danger. This is a color that wants us to be alive and stay alive. This is why the color red is also associated with the root chakra and its support of survival.

While the theme and goal of the foot chakras are *to be*, the primary essence of the root chakra is to *live*. Through the foot and root chakras you gain direct access to the energy of the Earth. It is drawn up through your feet and legs and is cultivated and utilized in the root chakra. This energy enables you to survive, live, and thrive.

Red gemstones interact with the root chakra and its purpose is to draw energy from the Earth and to live. Each gemstone color feeds a bit of its successor. Black connects the feet chakra energy to the root chakra and feeds grounding into the red realm of healing. It is this ability to ground and channel unlimited energy from the earth that forms the basis of red gemstone healing. Red gemstones will enhance the ability of the root chakra to perform efficiently, so the primary power and benefit of red gemstones is to help us maintain energy in the body. Effective energy flow in the body enhances three major areas of life: the ability to just live and function in life, react to any threats to your survival, and to spark passion.

Red Gemstones Help You Cultivate More . . .

Energy to Live

Without flowing, balanced, healthy energy, you cannot live. Energy helps you get out of bed in the morning. It helps you to work, earn money, pay your bills, and take care of your body. For immediate root chakra survival, you need to be able to function in your body, take responsibility for yourself, and take care of this home that is your body. This body "home" needs regular food, exercise, sleep, and sex to truly live, and the color red inspires all of this.

Red is likely associated with the root chakra because it is the color of blood. Blood and oxygen enable us to live. Red is a symbol of pure life essence.

Red inspires vitality. When you are drawing energy from the Earth, you feel alive and awake. The sight of red increases blood circulation. It "gets the heart pumping." Red gemstones help you have the energy to perform daily tasks. Use red gemstones to get you pumped up for the day or bring you out of the afternoon slump. Red stones can motivate you to start a task and see it through to the end.

Energy to Handle Survival Threats

Red is a color that captures attention. It inspires immediate action. There is a reason that red is used to indicate danger, for example, stop signs, red lights, and emergency vehicle lights. Red triggers you to stop and take notice of your surroundings. The alert color prepares you to potentially take action. It is also associated with internal calls to pay attention, such as, "red flags." The color red is associated with basic survival and aids in keeping you alive.

Red gemstones help you deal with physical crises and emergencies. Looking at the color red can stimulate the generation of adrenaline, which helps you take action. When in an active emergency, red grounds and stimulates you to prepare you for a fight or flight reaction. Red enables you to focus and react appropriately to save yourself and those around you.

For example, if you are in a car accident, you need focus to observe your condition and environment. Are you injured? Can you move? Is the car safe or do you need to get out? Can you call emergency services? Are there others in the car with you? What is their condition? Can they exit the car themselves or do they need to wait for an ambulance? These are all situations that require the grounding and energetic qualities of red gemstones.

Red stones can be kept in first aid kits, or in your car glove box, for emergency situations. It can be just a stone to be placed right in your pocket to support your efforts to get through the crisis, or a bracelet you can put on to wear while you react. During travel, keep a red gem in your carry-on bag. If you work in an emergency-related field, as a fire fighter, emergency dispatcher or technician, or work in an emergency room, red gem jewelry or pocket stones will support you during your workday. They will keep you focused and ready for action.

When it comes to survival, there is more to consider than immediate emergency issues. Red, and the root chakra, also support threats that are due to lack of care. Poor nutrition, lack of sleep, and insufficient movement can all lead to deterioration of the body and illness. Red gemstones help you recognize when you are overworked and are putting too much stress on your body. It supports the will to live.

Meditate with red stones if you know that you need to make corrections in your life to maintain good health. They will enable you to identify the areas of life that need to change. Eating too much fast food or coffee and it's causing stomach problems and poor sleep? Long work hours with little exercise can trigger stress-related illnesses. Adrenal fatigue is a condition that is caused by too much stress and too little self-care. Red stones can support you as you make the necessary changes to recover. It will stimulate the will to live and encourage you to be more aware about the status of your physical condition.

Red gemstones are very supportive when recovering from illness. They provide energy, grounding, and encourage healthy movement. Combined with proper diet, rest, mild exercise, and the treatment plan recommended by your doctor, red stones will stimulate your desire and willingness to heal.

Energy That Ignites Passion

Red is a symbol of sexuality and passion. It is associated with many stimulating and romantic items such as lipstick, lingerie, roses, and hair. It is a color that evokes the image of heat and fire. Although associated with the Earth, red can also have a hot, flaming effect on your personal energy. It can spark intensity of passion in many areas of your life.

When you are passionate about something, you are completely absorbed. You can direct your full energy toward it. While survival depends on your will to live, passion provides a reason to live. Red increases your ability to enjoy good wine, beautiful music, and the ability to be immersed in what you are passionate about. This color inspires a true "lust for life" that keeps us engaged, active, and rooted here in this life.

Red gemstones will help you enjoy the good things in life. Sit with red stones if you are feeling less interest in your hobbies and interests. It can reveal why you are feeling disconnected from them. Maybe you need to switch something up to ignite your interest again.

Allow the red gems to bring any energetic blocks to the surface. It could be that your current running path is getting boring and you should seek out new paths. You could try a different yoga teacher, read a new genre of books, or go to a sporting event live instead of watching it on TV. Maybe you need an entirely new hobby altogether. Wear red gems and observe what you encounter in your daily life. Allow yourself to be open to new possibilities and experiment. Let red help you rediscover what makes life worth living for.

There is passion for life and passion for the body. We need both. Sex is a way to keep the body's energy heightened and flowing. It amplifies physical, emotional, and energetic sensations in the body. Sex releases stress, encourages restful sleep, and can bring a real joy into life. Ensuring that you have a healthy intimate life, even by yourself, is important to maintaining true vitality and balanced energy.

Add red gemstones to your bedroom to help bring a spark to your sex life. If you've been in a relationship for a long time and your intimate life feels stale, red gems can remind you of what your partner's sexy traits are. For brand-new relationships, red stones can get your sex life off to a fiery start. Grid red gemstones on your nightstand or dresser to attract stimulating, flowing energy in your room. Bring red gemstones on vacation if you want to ignite the flames in your hotel room. Wear red gemstone jewelry during dates to heighten the excitement of the evening. Red gemstones will help you treat your energy and your body very well.

Signs You Need More RED Gemstone Energy

Try to incorporate red gemstones into your daily crystal healing practice if you are experiencing the following symptoms or occurrences in your life:

- Lack of physical energy and lethargy
- Inability to get quality sleep
- Beloved hobbies hold lesser interest
- Lack of sex drive, or aversion to sex
- Bored and apathetic on a regular basis
- No interest in engaging in life
- Poor nutrition
- The need to get work done but lacking in motivation
- Adrenal fatigue
- Chronic illness
- Professional work involving emergencies: emergency medical technician, emergency room staff, emergency dispatcher, search and rescue, etc.

RED GEMSTONES FOR ENERGY MAINTENANCE

These red stones provide the spark to ignite and refresh your personal energy, but also the unique supportive benefits listed below. Study these additional healing properties to help you identify the most appropriate stone to assist you.

Catlinite – Stone of the Ancestors: This is a stone that has been long used in Native American rituals. It helps you connect with your spirit guides and is a powerful stone for increasing the positive energy of rituals. This stone lets you see the sacred in everyday occurrences. It helps you to be at peace in the moment and connect deeply to the energy of ancestral and Earth energy.

Garnet – Stone of Renewal: Garnet removes negativity of all forms from our body and chakras and transmutes the energy to a beneficial state. It helps with emotional, spiritual, and physical regeneration. Garnet assists with purification, cleansing, and detoxification, and helps everything become fresh and new. Garnet also increases love, devotion, warmth, and understanding in relationships.

Mookaite – Stone of New Experiences and Adventure: It helps you to center so you can face change and new experiences calmly. It helps you to recognize all of the possibilities available and make wise choices. It will help you trust your instincts and abilities. Mookaite guides you intuitively toward your destiny. It provides enthusiasm and motivation to achieve your goals.

Red Aventurine – Stone of Action: All Aventurine balances and restores the energies within us and protects from energetic attachments. Red Aventurine in particular is a stone that stimulates your motivation to take action to bring your dreams to life. This stone encourages you to your individuality and uniqueness. It enables you to see problems as exciting challenges and not be discouraged when things aren't going as planned.

Red Calcite – Stone of Energy: All Calcite is a powerful cleanser and amplifier of energy. Red Calcite boosts energy, optimism, and motivation. It provides renewed flow of stagnant energy and provides an energetic "reset." It helps to dissolve energetic blockages that are impeding energy flow within the body.

Red Jasper – Stone of Energy and Protection: Red Jasper gets you going on days you need a little extra boost and the ability to stay focused no matter what the day throws at you. It is also worn to help promote independence and a sense of responsibility. Red Jasper is incredibly useful for multitasking and the motivation to get a job done.

Red Quartz – Stone of Vitality: This quartz ignites your energy and lust for life. It lifts physical energy, giving you momentum to take on tasks with enthusiasm. Use this stone to get ready for work in the morning, ward off an afternoon slump, or get ready for an evening out.

Red Tiger's Eye – Stone of Motivation and Stimulation: Adds vitality and passion to any endeavor. This stone boosts physical energy and inspires you to take action. If you are feeling lethargic or unmotivated to start a task, this gemstone will remind you of your purpose. Keeps one from feeling disconnected when working with higher goals. It stimulates your sex life and sense of romance.

Red Tourmaline (Rubellite) – Stone of Interaction: This crystal boosts physical energy and strengthens our ability to love. It is very useful for balancing all of your social skills and having the energy to maneuver large gatherings of people without feeling drained.

Ruby – Stone of Energy and Passion: This gemstone encourages energy, motivation, passion, and creativity. Ruby encourages you to follow your bliss while still setting realistic goals. It is incredibly protective, provides a shield against psychic attack, and shines hope in dark situations. Be careful, as Ruby tends to bring up the negative emotions and experiences we have been denying, to enable us to work through them and release them.

GEMSTONE MEDITATION FOR ENERGY MAINTENANCE

This is a guided meditation designed specifically to work with cultivating the energetic benefits of red gemstones. If you feel in need of more energy, enthusiasm, and passion, then identify a red gemstone and try this crystal meditation. Go at your own pace, as you feel comfortable. The more familiar you are with the energy of your gemstone, then the less time you may need to meditate to attain the benefits.

1. First, locate a red gemstone to use during this meditation.
2. Find a comfortable place to sit. For this meditation you will need to sit as close to the ground as possible. The root chakra draws energy from the earth, so try to minimize the distance between the two; however, comfort is important so a chair is fine if that is what you need. It can be inside or outside, as long as you can sit comfortably for about ten to twenty minutes.
3. Hold the red gemstone in your nondominant hand. This is your receiving hand that will take in the energy of the crystal.
4. Close your eyes and begin to take slow deep breaths.
5. Bring your awareness to where your legs and sitting bones are touching the floor or ground. Take a moment to feel the seat underneath you. You are completely supported and protected by the entire Earth underneath you.

6. Bring your attention to your body and take note of how your body, mind, emotions, and energy feel right now. Don't try to fix, change, or judge any experience, just take note. Be IN your body and see how it feels.

7. Check in with how your level of energy feels right now. Are you tired or alert? Are you feeling bored or interested?

8. Now take a minute to feel the stone in your hand. Take note of its weight, smoothness, texture, and how it feels as you hold it.

9. Imagine a bright sphere of energy forming in your hip region. It may be difficult at first to hold this visual, but it will get easier with practice.

10. Then imagine the sphere of energy in your hips starting to pull up energy from the Earth. Receive this energy and allow the sphere to grow and get brighter.

11. Then let the energy flow all throughout your body. Notice how it feels to have this energy immersing your body.

12. As you breathe in, allow the energy to flow up your body. As you exhale, watch the energy flow down your body. Continue to move the energy with your breath. Keep up this energetic flow exercise for a minute or two.

13. Notice how your level of energy feels right now. Are you more awake and ready to engage in life?

14. Let this energy gather again in your hip region. Imagine it now as a burning campfire. As the flames flicker it is turning up the level of stimulation in your life. If at any time it feels like you are holding too much energy, visualize the excess just flowing back down into the earth.

15. Imagine yourself now, completely awake, alive and present in the moment. Sit with this visualization as long as you feel comfortable.

16. After a few minutes, bring your awareness back to your breath and body. How does your body, mind, emotions, or energy feel now? Has anything changed since the beginning of the meditation? Don't try to force anything. It may take several meditation sessions to notice real change, but take note of anything. Journaling is especially helpful during this process.

17. Then release the imagery and come back to your breath. Just breathe and feel the Earth underneath your feet.

18. Take a few final deep breaths.

19. When you feel ready, open your eyes.

20. Take a few minutes to journal about your experience.

ORANGE | CREATION

CHAPTER 10

ORANGE GEMSTONES | CREATION

THE COLOR ORANGE is one that catches our attention and invites us to see the beauty in life. It is the color of fruit, blossoms, pumpkins, and fall. It displays the liveliness of nature. Orange energy is about taking in the wonders of life, participating in the exchange of creative and emotional energy, and contributing to the fullness of life. The energy of red encourages us to live and survive, but the color orange inspires us to enjoy life and experience its beauty.

Orange also stimulates the sacral chakra. This chakra relates to the element of water. Orange energy is open and flowing, like a river, a shower, or the rain downhill during a storm. It moves with grace around the obstacles of life. Orange helps energy and emotions flow naturally and freely throughout your body. It relieves tension, frustration, and constriction.

This is an energy that wants you to actively participate in your life. This participation and contribution are achieved by engaging with others and adding something to the collective of life. Orange supports those who desire to create and make something that didn't previously exist.

The energy of orange gemstones is open, flowing, and brings things to life. Orange is a color that helps us cultivate beauty and joy, inspires us to bring ideas to fruition, and to create life through passion.

Orange Gemstones Help You Cultivate More . . .

Sense of Beauty and Joy

Orange is a color that lifts the mood. It inspires happiness and joy. Orange encourages a sense of humor and the ability to let our emotions flow with unabated laughter. This color promotes optimism and seeing the silver lining during difficult situations. Orange helps us to recognize and acknowledge the beauty all around us. If your life is feeling stagnant or routine, get your energy flowing by meditation with an orange gemstone, such as Orange Calcite or Carnelian. It will help you rediscover the things in life that bring you joy. Maybe it is a good cup of coffee while you sit outside in the morning, a walk on your favorite trail, or the way fresh, clean sheets feel when you settle into bed. Orange gemstones are perfect to use when writing in a gratitude journal. It guides you through your day to identify those moments that you feel grateful for.

It may feel good to laugh, but it feels even better to laugh with friends. Orange is a color that promotes community and friendship. This is a color that helps us be more social and to appreciate the emotions that flow between two people. Sunstone is a phenomenal stone to unveil the social side of our being and is supportive for introverts as they venture into group situations. Orange helps us to share our feelings with others and to appreciate the help and support of others.

Like biting into a ripe, juicy orange, this color invites us to live life to the fullest, to take in experiences and to enjoy them. It stimulates vitality, enthusiasm, and curiosity in life. Orange encourages the inner child to come out, play, and have fun. No wonder it is one of the colors of Halloween. It is a night when children, and some adults, use their imagination, dress up, and indulge in candy. Orange reassures us that pleasure is to be embraced, not avoided. Wear or carry orange crystals when you are seeking to invite more fun and play into your life. You can take it with you on a spontaneous adventure or on vacation to remind you to relax, let your hair down, and have some fun.

Inspiration and the Ability to Create

Orange nurtures your willingness to be inspired and bring new creations to life. This applies to anyone who creates, such as artists, inventors, designers, writers, and anyone who makes something. Often when you are experiencing an artistic block or a lack of ideas, it is because of trying too hard to "think" of something. Trying to control the creative process acts as a dam in the waters of orange energy. Working with orange stones enables you to set your thinking mind aside and allow ideas and artistic energy to arise naturally.

If you are experiencing creator's block, or feel that you have lost your muse, sit in a quiet space with an orange gem before you start in on your work. Try to let go of the thinking mind that is trying so hard. Release the need to know and allow an open space for the universe to fill with new and beautiful images. Sit as long as you can, and when you feel ready, come to your workstation and just start making something. Or continue on that project that has felt stagnant. Just begin and allow the flow to happen.

Try an orange gemstone meditation at a location that inspires you, like a museum, bookstore, library, concert, garden, and see what arises while you are surrounded by the works of other creators. Wear or carry an orange gemstone to your favorite inspiring place and just watch, feel, and take in your environment. This method can bring new life and freshness to our own projects and creations.

The energy of orange also inspires you to stop and look at the beauty all around you. If life is feeling dull, stagnant, or just too rushed, this color invites us to stop and enjoy what we consider fun, beautiful, and soul soothing. Too much of the same routine will cause energetic blocks which lead to a lack of motivation and exhaustion. If you are not feeding and nurturing your soul, you won't be inspired or energized to bring forth your own work.

Take an orange gemstone to a place that you enjoy. Have a nice drink at a concert, take a walk through a botanical garden, sit at the beach, or just relax in a place, outside of your home, that reminds you that life should be enjoyed. Breathe, sit, watch, and feel the energy of life around you. Maybe bring a journal or sketchpad to capture any ideas that arise.

The Environment to Reproduce

Creation also refers to your own living ability to reproduce and create life. Not only can you bring forth art, music, architecture, and new innovations, but you can bring a new person into this world. Orange gemstones support you during conception and pregnancy as you perform the ultimate act of creation.

Fertility can be greatly influenced by your energetic, emotional, and mental states. Often the lack of ability to conceive is because of holding onto the pressure to conceive, stress of everyday life, or emotional wounds that are causing fear regarding pregnancy. All of these energetic influences can cause the body to resist conception. There are many instances of parents who can't conceive, but almost immediately after adopting a child, get pregnant.

To cultivate a relaxed, open, and willing energy to conceive, sit regularly with an orange gemstone. Send the idea of pregnancy out to the universe, the divine, or your spirit guides, and remain in a quiet, still contemplation. Watch what arises for you during this meditation. Is it fear of parenthood? Too much attachment to pregnancy? Worry about the change in your lifestyle? See what comes up for you and consider it. This is a good time to journal so you can watch for recurring issues and work them out on paper. Orange gemstones can help you identify what is blocking your energy to conceive, so you can address it directly.

Orange is a color that supports developing healthy relationships with others. Healthy sexual relationships thrive with honesty, compassion, touch, and fun. If there is tension in your relationship, orange gemstones assist in having open conversations about issues. Orange will stimulate a relationship that is stagnant and encourage including more fun.

Use orange stones in your bedroom to create the optimal energy for sex and conception. Orange is a color that stimulates sexual desire and can help you release any expectations about conception that are holding you back. Orange invites you to let your body relax into the pleasure of sex and let the thinking mind and constricting emotions take a back seat. Just be with your partner, enjoy them, and let the pleasurable energy flow.

Signs You Need More ORANGE Gemstone Energy

Try to incorporate orange gemstones into your daily crystal healing practice if you are experiencing the following symptoms or occurrences in your life:

- Lack of creativity or writer's block
- Difficulty starting a new project
- Unable to see the beauty in life
- Mental rigidity, or things have to be a certain way
- Uncomfortable "letting loose" or having fun
- Difficulty expressing emotions
- Low mood or depression

- Difficulty forming or committing to relationships
- Habit of being in unhealthy, abusive, or codependent relationships
- Revulsion to being touched
- Are trying to conceive
- Are currently pregnant
- Desire a more fun and spontaneous sex life
- Fear of change or of trying something new

ORANGE GEMSTONES FOR CREATION

These orange stones inspire creativity and passion, but also provide the unique supportive benefits listed below. Study these additional healing properties to help you identify the most appropriate stone to assist you.

Amber – Stone of Optimism: This fossilized tree sap is a powerful energetic cleanser. It absorbs negative energies and transmutes them into bright, uplifting energy. This stone increases the drive to create and achieve your goals. It brings hope, optimism, and eases depression.

Carnelian – The Artist's Stone: Carnelian awakens hidden talents and gifts. Carnelian is a stone of creativity and inspiration in all forms of art, particularly drama and theater. It awakens curiosity and bolsters the courage of shy people. Wear carnelian when you do public speaking as it inspires courage and eloquence. Carnelian also transmutes negative energy into positive! It is also believed to enhance and stimulate sexual activity.

Fire Agate – Stone of Security: Fire Agate is extremely protective. It connects you to the Earth to provide a deep sense of safety. The fire dispels fear and instills a sense of security. It boosts energy and passion. Fire Agate encourages introspection and the resolving of inner problems.

Hessonite Garnet – Stone of Renewal: Garnet removes negativity of all forms from our body and chakras and transmutes the energy to a beneficial state. It helps with emotional, spiritual, and physical regeneration, so everything feels fresh and new. Hessonite Garnet boosts self-esteem and eliminates feelings of inferiority. It helps to ease a guilty conscious if you aren't truly to blame.

Orange Calcite – Stone of Optimism: All Calcite is a powerful cleanser and amplifier of energy. Orange Calcite is a stone that uplifts energy and potential. It particularly reduces fear and helps you overcome depression. It helps you have a more positive and hopeful outlook on life.

Orange Selenite – Stone of Renewal: Just like White Selenite, Orange Selenite is extremely cleansing. This crystal works closely with the sacral chakra and helps to clear out old ideas, habits, and rooted belief systems that are causing us to remain stuck. This helps clear out old energy and make room for fresh new ideas and creativity.

Peach Aventurine – Stone of Soothing: All Aventurine is very healing, restores energies within us, and protects from energetic attachments. Peach Aventurine is very soothing and calming. It alleviates shyness and helps you be more at ease around people. This stone also boosts creativity and quiets the mind in preparation for meditation.

Peach Moonstone – Stone of the Child: All Moonstone is nurturing as its core benefit. Peach Moonstone is especially supportive for children. It alleviates fear and strengthens a sense of security. This stone helps children feel more confident, creative, and encourages authenticity.

Poppy Jasper – Stone of Resolution: This stone assists us in seeing problems before they occur. It encourages self-honesty and the courage to step forward to fix our own issues before they grow out of control. This stone brings insight to conflict and shows us how to diffuse a situation effectively. Poppy Jasper also helps to rectify unjust situations and reminds you to treat others fairly. This stone also stimulates fire, creativity, and sexuality in your life.

Sardonyx – Stone of Strength and Protection: This is a powerful stone to have around the house because it will strengthen the energetic protection of a home. It discourages people from trespassing on your property. Sardonyx boosts inner strength, integrity, willpower, and energy. It strengthens relationships, attracts friends and fortune. It also helps to alleviate depression.

Sunstone – Stone of Personal Power: Sunstone encourages leadership, courage, inner conviction, self-discipline, and abundance. This gemstone allows you to invite abundance and generosity into your life. The more you send out to support others, even more will return. It also cleanses and strengthens the aura and supports you as you cut energetic attachments within your aura.

GEMSTONE MEDITATION FOR CREATION

This is a guided meditation designed specifically to work with cultivating the energetic benefits of orange gemstones. If you feel in need of more fun, creativity, and emotional expression, then identify an orange gemstone and try this crystal meditation. Go at your own pace, as you feel comfortable. The more familiar you are with the energy of your gemstone, the less time you may need to meditate to attain the benefits.

1. First, locate an orange gemstone to use during this meditation.
2. Find a comfortable place to sit. You can sit on a cushion on the floor, a chair, or directly on the ground outside. Make sure you can sit tall and comfortably for about ten to twenty minutes.
3. Hold the orange gemstone in your nondominant hand. This is your receiving hand that will take in the energy of the crystal.
4. Close your eyes and begin to take slow deep breaths.
5. Bring your awareness to where your legs and sitting bones are touching the floor or ground. Take a moment to feel the seat underneath you. You are completely supported and protected by the entire Earth underneath you.
6. Bring your attention to your body and take note of how your body, mind, emotions, and energy feel right now. Don't try to fix, change, or judge any experience, just take note. Be IN your body and see how it feels.

7. Check in with how your emotions feel right now. Can you sit with your emotions comfortably, or does it feel difficult to look at them?
8. Now take a minute to feel the stone in your hand. Take note of its weight, smoothness, texture, and how it feels as you hold it.
9. Imagine a bright orange sphere of energy forming in your hip region. It may be difficult at first to hold this visual, but it will get easier with practice.
10. Then imagine the sphere of energy in your hips blossoming and growing larger until it encompasses you completely.
11. Let the energy swirl and flow within and around you.
12. Notice how it feels to have this energy flowing throughout your body, dissolving tension, relaxing your muscles, and releasing any thoughts you might be holding onto.
13. As the energy flows around you, slowly move your upper body like the swirling orange energy flow. Notice where you move easily, and where you seem stuck.
14. Slowly stop your movement and sit with a still mind and body, but imagine the energy still flowing through and around you. Invite the universe, the divine, or your spirit guides to gift you with inspiration, ideas for incorporating more fun, and to release your control. Sit with this open intention for several minutes.
15. Bring your attention to any emotional issues you've been experiencing lately. How deeply can you feel your emotions? Let the orange energy flow through this situation, dissolving any barriers you've built up around

it. Let the emotion expand and flow. You are protected by the energy of the earth you sit upon, and you can experience and feel these emotions safely.

16. Notice how your body feels right now. Are you more relaxed, at ease, and can you breathe easier? If you are still holding tightly somewhere in your body or heart, continue to let the energy flow.

17. After a few minutes, bring your awareness back to your breath and body. How do your body, mind, emotions, or energy feel now? Has anything changed since the beginning of the meditation? Don't try to force anything. It may take several meditation sessions to notice real change but take note of anything. Journaling is especially helpful during this process.

18. Then release the imagery and come back to your breath. Just breathe and feel the Earth underneath your feet.

19 Take a few final deep breaths.

20. When you feel ready, open your eyes.

21. Take a few minutes to journal about your experience.

BROWN | GROWTH

CHAPTER 11

BROWN GEMSTONES | GROWTH

Brown is a color that doesn't get much attention in the color healing arena, but it is vital to our health and development as a person and as a spiritual being. Brown is the color of rich, nourishing dirt that enables plants and trees to grow and thrive. June McLeod, in her book *Colour Psychology Today*, describes brown as "the soil in which everything grows." Brown is the color of wood, leather, and the comforts of home. It fosters a sense of stability and responsibility.

This color is a mix of red, yellow, and black. It stimulates the properties of both the root and solar plexus chakras. Brown provides the sense of security from the qualities of the black gemstones, the energetic boost from red stones, and the motivational benefits from yellow crystals. This works to nurture an environment ripe for growth and expansion. After we are rooted and focused from black and red gemstones, and orange stones have inspired us to live life and be creative, then brown encourages you to expand, grow, and develop into a more fully realized being. The color brown evokes the image of a great, tall tree expanding out into the sky. Much like the massive redwood trees in Northern California, so wide you could drive a car through a tunnel carved in the base of one of the trees.

The energy of brown gemstones enables us to determine our personal and spiritual path, cultivate financial stability, and open up to personal and professional growth and development.

Brown Gemstones Help You Cultivate More . . .

Acceptance of This Life as a Human

The human experience is one of learning. Of fully opening up to life and absorbing the lessons of this earthly existence. Brown gemstones support your soul in this physical incarnation so you can experience and learn from this human life.

Sometimes the ability to live life and gather learning experiences is hindered by a reluctance to actually be a part of the human experience. People can feel disconnected from their body, their human life, and wish to be somewhere else. This might be experienced as wanting to sleep and dream often, daydreaming of life in heaven or other dimensions, or just not feeling comfortable in your own skin. This can occur after near-death experiences but can also begin at birth and manifest as a lack of engagement in life.

Meditating with brown gemstones will help you realize there is a reason you were born into this body at this time. You have life lessons to learn and experience so your soul can grow and move further along in its journey. Meditating with brown crystals, such as Mahogany Obsidian, will allow you to come home to Mother Earth and the experience of living.

Responsibility and Financial Stability

If you find yourself in need of financial stability and security, then brown is a color to explore. It is soothing and reassuring if you are stressed about financial debts and responsibilities. Brown helps you understand the scope of your financial needs and figure out how to fulfill them.

Brown helps to cultivate a mindset that has strong common sense. A person who is practical, hardworking, and down-to-earth. Use brown gemstones when you need to invite more duty and responsibility in your life. Brown gemstones are perfect for one who is looking for a job as they aid you in exuding the energy of a committed and dedicated employee. Wear Brown Tourmaline during a job interview as it inspires within you an air of professionalism and determination.

If you're not sure what you want to do for a living, brown gemstones help you to discover a field you would excel at and enjoy. Brown aids you in committing to a profession, obtaining the necessary training, and pursuing the career you desire.

A Nurturing Environment to Develop

The color brown is warm and cozy, like our favorite chair or blanket. It helps us develop a sense of home and comfort when we are feeling lost and adrift. When we don't have the stability of a home, we won't feel secure enough to plant roots and grow. This doesn't necessarily mean a physical house but could also include a familiar city or community that makes us feel accepted and supported.

Brown energy provides a gently grounding sense of home that feeds a desire to *be more*. Brown crystals help us establish our footing and provide the nutrients and energy stability for us to release blocks and to develop. Brown assists with learning from the past and not repeating those behaviors or situations. Brown gems initiate the release of self-imposed limitations, blocking us from growing as a soul and a person. This color helps us look at decisions or situations with calm focus, detached from previous emotional baggage or habitual programming, to determine the best path forward.

Development could be practically, professionally, academically, or spiritually. It could involve learning a new skill, changing careers, starting therapy, or starting formal spiritual study. Brown encourages us to be determined and hardworking to achieve satisfying and fruitful growth. The energy of brown provides the stability and confidence to grow tall and wide like a large, shady oak tree. If you feel unsure about your next step in life, sitting with a brown gemstone such as Septarian or Petrified Wood will act as a compass and guide you in the right direction.

Signs You Need More BROWN Gemstone Energy

Try to incorporate brown gemstones into your daily crystal healing practice if you are experiencing the following symptoms or occurrences in your life:

- Indecision about your direction or goals in life
- Beginning school, training, or online classes
- Learning a new skill or hobby
- Not being sure what the purpose of existing is
- Not feeling comfortable in your human body
- Feeling adrift and in need of a home base
- Financial difficulties
- Needing employment

BROWN GEMSTONES FOR GROWTH AND DEVELOPMENT

These brown stones provide the nourishment for growth and development, but also the unique supportive benefits listed below. Study these additional healing properties to help you identify the most appropriate stone to assist you.

Bronzite – Stone of Stability: This stone is a protective and grounding stone, helping you to remain calm and decisive during chaotic situations. It helps you see the big picture, identify all of your options, and then take decisive action. Bronzite helps you enter into a state of stillness, which works well during meditation or crisis. This stone also protects against psychic attacks as it reflects any negative energy back to the originator.

Brown Tourmaline (Dravide) – Stone of Integration: This gem helps you to feel comfortable in your body during this human incarnation. It also helps strengthen relationships, communities, and helps you feel comfortable in large groups of people.

Chiastolite – Stone of Transition: This stone was historically used to ward off the "evil eye." It is still used to ward off dark energies and transmute negativity into lightness. This stone helps in the death and rebirth cycle, as well as out of body travel. It helps to loosen the attachment to the body to allow the soul to move freely. This is a comforting stone to hold during end of life situations (both for the dying and their loved ones) because it eases the transition and allows everyone to let go.

Dalmatian Stone – Stone of Integration and Play: This stone helps to ground your soul with your body. To remind you that you are a spiritual being on a human journey. If you are feeling disconnected or lethargic, Dalmatian Stone will help you to feel integrated and energized. It brings out the playful, childlike side of you so you can enjoy your adventure in this human body.

Mahogany Obsidian – Stone of Development: Stimulates growth of the physical, emotional, intellectual, and spiritual centers, and provides strength in times of need. Provides vitality to one's lifework and help with the fulfillment of goals.

Petrified Wood – Stone of Wisdom: This stone is formed when wood falls into water and absorbs metals and minerals. It is perfect for helping you find a mentor. Its deep connection to the past makes it a supportive stone for past life and soul work. This stone encourages spiritual evolution and development of inner wisdom.

Picture Jasper – Stone of Reflection: This stone provides the comfort of Mother Earth. It is said the picture in the jasper brings sacred messages to the viewer. It brings repressed memories and feelings to the surface to be acknowledged and healed. Once these issues are released, you retain the memory of them as life lessons along your path and avoid repeating mistakes.

Schalenblende – Stone of Resilience: Is grounding and very protective. It helps to regenerate energy and physical strength. It helps you absorb energy from the Earth to improve endurance. This stone supports you when you feel like you have almost exhausted your personal resources and can't handle any more. Encourages productive communication between people in conflict.

Septarian – Stone of Connection: This stone inspires cohesiveness among people. It stimulates a feeling of connection and compassion. It is very supportive within spiritual groups, if you're speaking to an audience, leading group discussion, or in a new social situation. This ancient creation encourages you to take care of the Earth. It is very useful during sound healing and rituals, such as drumming circles, sound bowls, and chanting.

Stromatolite – Stone of Life Lessons: This stone is formed from fossilized cyanobacteria and is one of the oldest stones on the Earth. It connects you deeply with ancestral guidance and the wisdom of the Earth. It assists with past-life work and enables you to use those lessons for future growth. It supports learning from past mistakes and allows you to easily let go of unhealthy situations, people, and habits.

Wonderstone – Stone of Tranquility: This stone is used to facilitate and reinforce the state of tranquility. It can be helpful in eliminating worries, allowing you to recognize that "worry" does not change a situation. It is an excellent stone for bringing mental clarity to any predicament and giving insight into the right course of action. It is an excellent meditation stone and enhances creativity. It also helps reduce or eliminate depression and anxiety, giving an overall sense of well-being.

GEMSTONE MEDITATION FOR GROWTH AND DEVELOPMENT

This is a guided meditation designed specifically to work with cultivating the energetic benefits of brown gemstones. If you feel in need of security in which to develop, then identify a brown gemstone and try this crystal meditation. Go at your own pace, as you feel comfortable. The more familiar you are with the energy of your gemstone, the less time you may need to meditate to attain the benefits.

1. First, locate a brown gemstone to use during this meditation.
2. Find a comfortable place to sit. You can sit on a cushion on the floor, a chair, or directly on the ground outside. Make sure you can sit tall and comfortably for about ten to twenty minutes.
3. Hold the brown gemstone in your nondominant hand. This is your receiving hand that will take in the energy of the crystal.

4. Close your eyes and begin to take slow deep breaths.
5. Bring your awareness to where your legs and sitting bones are touching the floor or ground. Take a moment to feel the seat underneath you. You are completely supported and protected by the entire Earth underneath you.
6. Bring your attention to your body and take note of how your body, mind, emotions, and energy feel right now. Don't try to fix, change, or judge any experience, just take note. Be IN your body and see how it feels.
7. Check in with how your emotions feel right now. Can you sit with your emotions comfortably, or does it feel difficult to look at them?
8. Now take a minute to feel the stone in your hand. Take note of its weight, smoothness, texture, and how it feels as you hold it.
9. Imagine roots growing down from your thighs and sitting bones deep into the ground beneath you. These roots will help you feel stable and grounded.
10. Then imagine drawing nurturing, vital energy from the Earth, up through the roots, and filling your entire body with light.
11. Imagine this light expanding and shining beyond your physical body.
12. Picture tree branches covered in lush, green leaves expanding out from your upper body as far as they can go.
13. As you breathe, allow your chest and lungs to open wide and accept in this nourishing air. Bring your shoulders back a little to expand your lung capacity.

14. Consider what in your life you would like to expand and grow just like the great tree you have become. What area of your life could use some attention and nourishment?

15. Imagine that aspect of your life and the ways in which it can manifest and grow. Feel confident in your ability to make that happen, to take the next step, and to work toward something new and fulfilling.

16. After a few minutes, bring your awareness back to your breath and body. How does your body, mind, emotions or energy feel now? Has anything changed since the beginning of the meditation? Don't try to force anything. It may take several meditation sessions to notice real change but take note of anything. Journaling is especially helpful during this process.

17. Then release the imagery and come back to your breath. Just breathe and feel the Earth underneath you.

18. Take a few final deep breaths.

19. When you feel ready, open your eyes.

20. Take a few minutes to journal about your experience.

YELLOW | CONFIDENCE

CHAPTER 12

YELLOW GEMSTONES | CONFIDENCE

YELLOW IS THE COLOR that brings light into our lives. It is the color of the bright sun that warms us and wakes us up in the morning. Just as the scent or taste of lemon perks us up and helps us feel more alert, so does yellow stimulate and drive our personal energy.

Yellow is linked to the solar plexus chakra (also referred to as the navel chakra) and is commonly referred to as the "power center." The solar plexus energy is associated with the fire element. When stimulated by the fire element you shine bright like flames or the rays of the sun. You can feel tall and glorious as a sunflower facing into the dazzling rays of the sun. This is an energy that lifts up our confidence, and encourages optimism and happiness.

At wavelength 580nm, yellow is the color that stands out to our eyes the most. Because of this quality, it is used primarily to catch one's attention. Yellow is used for warning road signs, letting us know where the crosswalks are, dangerous turns, or animal crossings. Taxis are painted yellow to enable us to easily see them on the road and hail a cab. In 1962, the original highlighter was invented. It was a brilliant, bright shade of yellow, designed so you could quickly find the lines in a book you had highlighted. Post-it Notes were invented in 1980 and also used the color yellow to catch the eye. People could jot a note, stick it on a board or in a book, and it would not be lost in a crown of papers. Yellow invites people to *notice*. After the color brown has enabled us to plant roots and begin to grow, yellow inspires us to step forward and be noticed in this life.

Joanne and Arielle Eckstut state in their book, *The Secret Language of Colors,* "In Buddhist Tantra literature... yellow is the color used to represent things on the rise: from wealth and health to knowledge and wisdom." Yellow enables us to step forward, be noticed, and achieve our dreams. All of the energies of yellow combine to help us develop strong confidence, the ability to stand strong on our own two feet, and the motivation to take advantage of opportunities when they arise.

Yellow Gemstones Help You Cultivate More...

Confidence

One of the emotions that blocks our satisfaction and abundance is self-doubt. This is a sensation that plagues many people in the Western world. It is extremely common for us to feel self-doubt, self-criticism, and experience low self-esteem. I have often felt that most people do not treat themselves as a friend, but as an adversary to overcome. It is this self-doubt that prevents us from fully experiencing life and taking advantage of the many opportunities for growth, development, and abundance. Doubt convinces us that we aren't good enough, qualified, deserving, or ready to take the next step toward success. When we build confidence, we overcome doubt.

Confidence isn't overblown ego. It is the ability to trust, respect, and love yourself. You trust in your abilities and choices. You respect yourself and honor the need to take care of yourself. As a confident person, you treat yourself as a friend. You encourage yourself to try and pick yourself back up with care and compassion if you don't succeed. This is a state of being that can easily be cultivated with consistent care and meditation.

Yellow gemstones help amplify this process. Yellow energy serves as a pick-me-up, inspiring optimism, self-esteem, and strength of ego. The energy of yellow crystals, such as Honey Calcite and Citrine, help us shine bright like the sun and stand tall like the beautiful sun flowers. They give you the confidence to stand out in the crowd.

If you feel yourself experiencing low self-esteem, working with yellow gemstones will help you boost your confidence, release the nagging thoughts of doubt, and start recognizing your strengths and talents. As I was writing my first book, I was plagued by doubt. I questioned my skill, expertise, and even my own theories. I would regularly meditate with Gold Tiger's Eye to release the grasp that "Imposter's Syndrome" had on me and to recognize all the truth and wisdom I was offering.

Use yellow whenever you need a boost of confidence. Wear or carry Citrine during a job interview, presentation, proposal, business negotiation, asking for an opportunity, or working on an important project. It will enable your true, beautiful self to shine right through any self-doubt or judgment.

Personal Power

An aspect of being that falls hand-in-hand with our confidence is our sense of personal power. This is our ability to stand up for what we believe, define and enforce personal boundaries, and to take care of ourselves when needed. Christian Valnet said in his book, *Chromotherapy: The Power of Colors*, that yellow is the color of "personal affirmation and the exercise of individual power." With personal power, we can regulate the give and take in social interactions. You can confidently discuss your opinion rather than try to figure out what the people around you would be pleased to hear. Personal power recognizes that you can't please everyone and it's exhausting to try.

Those who lack confidence and personal power also lack the

ability to make authentic decisions. They make choices they feel will make other people happy. Without individual power it is hard to say, "No." Inability to set personal boundaries can lead to exhaustion and burn out. A person may feel like it's rude to refuse, or that people will think poorly of them, so they accept every request.

Not enforcing personal boundaries will quickly drain your energy reserves. All of your time and energy goes into activities for other people with little to no time left for satisfying and fulfilling enjoyment for self. Or even time to rest and recuperate. It's important to give ourselves the respect and self-care we deserve and require to maintain our health.

Working with yellow gemstones will help you decide which requests you genuinely want to accept and which ones you do not have the time or desire for. They will help you stand up for your opinions, beliefs, and actions. Yellow gemstones feel empowering and strengthening. They will increase vitality and joy because you function in a state of strength and balance with other people.

Motivation

Yellow is a color that stimulates our appetite and hunger. It is linked to the fire in the solar plexus and stomach region. It stokes not just physical hunger, but the hunger of our ambitions as well. When you have confidence and inner power, you can focus on what you want out of life. You can confidently state your dreams and aspirations out loud. It alleviates fear of change and inspires a desire for curiosity and change.

You no longer doubt your abilities and can confidently apply for that new job, start writing that book, ask the intriguing person on a date, or head to the gym to improve your health. You know you can be *more* and are willing to make the effort.

Yellow gemstones are particularly supportive when you want

to make a change or take the next step in working toward a goal. They help you figure out the best way to proceed and increase your motivation to get started. Yellow crystals ignite the spark within to shine brighter and reach for the stars.

Signs You Need More YELLOW Gemstone Energy

Try to incorporate yellow gemstones into your daily Crystal Wisdom practice if you are experiencing the following symptoms or occurrences in your life.

- Self-critical thoughts
- Low self-esteem
- Fear of taking chances
- A difficulty saying "No"
- Defining and enforcing personal boundaries
- Working longer hours on tasks you don't enjoy
- Exhaustion and lack of motivation
- Hesitation to state your opinions, desires, or preferences
- Deference to everyone else's choices
- Trouble making decisions
- A continued wish for something but lack of effort to achieve it
- Feeling stagnant and bored in life

YELLOW GEMSTONES FOR CONFIDENCE

These yellow stones increase confidence and your sense of self-worth, but also provide the unique supportive benefits listed below. Study these additional healing properties to help you identify the most appropriate stone to assist you.

Bumblebee Jasper – Stone of New Beginnings: This stone helps you to accept change and gracefully let go of what is no longer serving you. It helps you to see new possibilities, take new risks, and go on adventures. It boosts the confidence to move forward and allows you to make wise decisions that are not emotionally reactive.

Citrine – Stone of Abundance: Citrine is a powerful stone that never needs cleansing. It automatically transmutes any negative energy into radiant light and protects the aura from attack. This gemstone also encourages great success, abundance, and generosity. It is a wonderful tool for manifesting your dreams.

Fossil Coral – Stone of Courage: This agatized stone carries with it the ancient energy of the life it used to contain. It helps you overcome any hesitation to speak up. It grants courage and confidence in social situations. You can also develop wisdom about business and promote career success.

Gold Topaz – Stone of Inspiration: This gemstone lifts you up as it helps to recharge your physical, mental, emotional, and spiritual batteries! This stone helps you recognize your own abilities and put them to best use. It encourages drive, confidence, and overcoming barriers to your success. It also helps you connect with the source of your divinity and you can use it to follow your highest life path.

Golden Healer Quartz – The Healer's Stone: This is an extremely high vibrational stone that brings healing ability to the next level. This gemstone connects you to all of the supportive energy sources and guides to enable you to effectively channel the pure healing power. This quartz inspires confidence in your abilities as a healer and enables you to bring more healing to the world.

Honey Calcite – Stone of Confidence: All Calcite is a powerful cleanser and amplifier of energy. Honey Calcite helps you acknowledge your own personal power and recognize how to use it wisely. It helps in developing leadership skills. This gemstone increases feelings of self-worth, confidence, and courage. It supports you in overcoming obstacles to your goals.

Tiger's Eye – Stone of Sun and Earth: This is a stone that allows you to see the divine in your everyday life. It keeps you grounded while you reach to the heavens. If you feel "spacey," then Tiger Eye will help you feel more centered. Tiger Eye is also a stone that allows you to manifest your personal power, increases motivation, and confidence.

Yellow Aventurine – Stone of Self-Worth: All Aventurine is very healing, restores energies within us, and protects from energetic attachments. Yellow Aventurine is very effective at resolving self-confidence issues. This stone helps you acknowledge and own your own value and contribution to the world. It assists people who are indecisive and helps them trust their intuition.

Yellow Calcite – Stone of Expansion: All Calcite is a powerful cleanser and amplifier of energy. Yellow Calcite is particularly uplifting and motivating. It helps deepen meditation, calm the mind, and achieve the experience of expanding past this physical body.

Yellow Jasper – Stone of Travel: This is an energizing stone that protects during spiritual work and travel (both physical and astral). Yellow Jasper was historically used as a protective talisman. This stone brings positive energy to body, mind, and soul. It is a grounding stone, but encourages confidence when you are feeling overwhelmed or out of your comfort zone.

GEMSTONE MEDITATION FOR CONFIDENCE

This is a guided meditation designed specifically to work with evoking confidence and motivation with yellow gemstones. If you feel in need of a boost of confidence, to release critical thoughts, or to step forward and take a chance, then identify a yellow gemstone and try this crystal meditation. Go at your own pace, as you feel comfortable. The more familiar you are with the energy of your gemstone, the less time you may need to meditate to attain the benefits.

1. First, locate a yellow gemstone to use during this meditation.
2. Find a comfortable place to sit. You can sit on a cushion on the floor, a chair, or directly on the ground outside. Make sure you can sit tall and comfortably for about ten to twenty minutes.
3. Hold the yellow gemstone in your nondominant hand. This is your receiving hand that will take in the energy of the crystal.
4. Close your eyes and begin to take slow deep breaths.

5. Bring your awareness to where your legs and sitting bones are touching the floor or ground. Take a moment to feel the seat underneath you. You are completely supported and protected by the entire Earth underneath you.
6. Bring your attention to your body and take note of how your body, mind, emotions, and energy feel right now. Don't try to fix, change, or judge any experience, just take note. Be IN your body and see how it feels.
7. Now take a minute to feel the stone in your hand. Take note of its weight, smoothness, texture, and how it feels as you hold it.
8. Pull your shoulders back a little to open your solar plexus area.
9. Imagine a small, bright sun growing just underneath your rib cage.
10. Envision the rays of this sun expanding outward past your physical body. Feel the warm rays of the sunlight.
11. You now accept and exude confidence, strength, and stand openly in your space of power.
12. Bring to mind the situation you need support with.
13. Imagine the sunlight dissolving any fears and doubts.
14. Remind yourself that you CAN do this. You have the strength, desire, and ability to achieve your dreams. You can stand up for your opinions, and you can enforce your personal boundaries.
15. Imagine you are doing what you need to do, because you CAN and WILL. Sit with this energy of strength for a minute or two.

16. After a few minutes, bring your awareness back to your breath and body. How does your body, mind, emotions, or energy feel now? Has anything changed since the beginning of the meditation? Don't try to force anything. It may take several meditation sessions to notice real change but take note of anything. Journaling is especially helpful during this process.
17. Then release the imagery and come back to your breath. Just breathe and feel the seat underneath you.
18. Take a few final deep breaths.
19. When you feel ready, open your eyes.
20. Take a few minutes to journal about your experience.

GREEN | HEALING

CHAPTER 13

GREEN GEMSTONES | HEALING

GREEN STRIKES THE EYE in a perfectly balanced manner. It requires the least work for our eyes to see, so it is soothing and calming to view. June McLeod says that green is "neutral, reconciling and soothing, the mid-point of all colors."

The color green also lands on the mid-point of the chakra system at the heart chakra. It shares the heart with the color pink. As the center of the chakra body, the heart chakra provides a bridge between the lower and upper chakras. An open heart chakra enables the energy to flow freely throughout the body. The heart is a space of balance, peace, and harmony in our energetic system.

The heart chakra is also associated with the element of air. Air can be soft, soothing, and calming, like a nice cool breeze on a warm day. The energy of air provides a sense of freshness and clears stagnancy. A breath of fresh air can make us feel awake and alive. The air in a green forest smells fresh and clean. Green and air leave us with a feeling of renewal, of spring cleaning, and of a time of rejuvenation.

Green is the most prevalent color in nature. It is associated with plant life on the Earth. It symbolizes abundance, growth, and beginning anew. Green represents life and connects us to the vital, healing energy of the Earth. Those drawn to green are often seeking heart healing, compassion, and harmony in their relationships.

Green Gemstones Help You Cultivate More . . .

Healing

Green is the color of healthy, living plants. Life on Earth depends on green plants as a mechanism to provide clean, fresh oxygen from carbon dioxide. Where there is green, there is also water and a nourishing place for food to grow. A "green thumb" is a phrase used for someone who is talented in growing plants, flowers, and gardens.

The vitality of green enables us to tap into the inherent healing abilities within. Working with green gemstones helps us heal emotional wounds whether they are recent or stem from far in the past. If you are recovering from heartache or betrayal, Green Aventurine will provide a safe, healing space for you to process and recover from your heart wounds. It will help you release attachment to the pain and feel secure enough to love again.

Green is also a color that helps us encourage healing on all levels of our being. The position on the color spectrum and the chakra system reflects its ability to foster balance. The balancing nature of green inspires feelings of rest, balance, restoration, and rejuvenation. No matter what we are healing from, an illness, injury, or deep emotional pain, green works to bring our systems back to a natural state. It eases the pain of extreme emotions and sensations to encourage a calming and soothing experience. Having a green gemstone with you during any healing process will keep you calm, hopeful, and in the best frame of mind to heal.

Green has become a sign of Earth healing and is the color identifying something as "eco-friendly." It is the color of environmentalism. Working with green gemstones like Moss and Tree Agate, or Unakite, encourage a desire to heal damage to the Earth. Meditating with green crystals will enforce the importance of taking care of the Earth and help you uncover ideas for how you can help.

Compassion

Green is also the color of healers and it is no surprise that it is also the color of medical scrubs. At the core nature of the healer is a desire to help others, to ease their pain and suffering. Healing taps into our inherent sense of compassion and empathy for other beings.

As the color of the heart center, green encourages us to tap into and expand our sense of compassion. It helps us increase feelings of kindness and benevolence to others. Our own healing and pain are a bridge to expanding our ability to feel compassion for another. Experiencing wounds helps us connect with others' suffering. We understand what they have been through. We can imagine and feel their pain. For example, do you remember when someone you cared for died? Can you recall the grief and sadness you experienced? When a neighbor's loved one dies, you are able to recall feeling the very same way. This shared pain experience helps us to understand that we're not all that different, regardless of if we disagree about some things. We have all experienced suffering, and we all wish to be free from suffering.

If you are having difficulty feeling sympathy for someone, or for a suffering community, hold a green stone such as Moldavite to enable you to tap into your well of empathy, to recall times when you too suffered, and to send them healing and love even if you do not understand the depth of their pain.

Patience and Harmony

Through compassion and empathy, we can work to strengthen patience and promote harmony in our lives. Impatience stems from frustration over a lack of control. With patience we can release the desire to control and just go with the flow of the situation. Patience connects us to the heart of other people, because when we are impatient it is often because we are waiting on another person. Maybe you are waiting for them to complete a task, respond to an email, complete their part of a project, or begin to behave differently. It is impossible to control everything and the more we become detached from that desire, the more peace and harmony we cultivate in our heart.

Bring Jade or another green gemstone with you when you know you may be triggered by impatience. Examples could be a meeting with a frustrating person, having to wait in a long line, or maneuvering through airports during travel. A green gem will not only enable you to be prepared in advance, but will ease and dissolve the feelings of frustration when they arise. These stones connect your heart to another, to your well of compassion, and bring a sense of ease, rather than struggle, in challenging situations.

Finally, green gemstones help bring harmony in relationships, especially when there are disagreements. Green reminds us of why we care for this person and brings your attention back to the importance of your relationships, instead of the topic of the disagreement. Although the color green represents jealousy, it can help us break free from feelings of jealousy. It reminds us that the other person is a human being as well and encourages compassion rather than envy. The connection of heart-to-heart awareness fosters harmony and peace in relationships.

Signs You Need More GREEN Gemstone Energy

Try to incorporate green gemstones into your daily Crystal Wisdom practice if you are experiencing the following symptoms or occurrences in your life.

- Recovering from a broken heart
- Feeling betrayed by someone you trusted
- Trying to heal from past traumas
- Recovering from an illness or injury

- Suffering from unrequited love
- Frequent impatience at others and life situations
- Difficulty feeling compassion for others
- A need for more understanding and harmony in a relationship
- Frustration or disagreement with someone you care about

GREEN GEMSTONES FOR HEALING

These green stones support your abilities to heal and recover on all levels, but also provide the unique supportive benefits listed below. Study these additional healing properties to help you identify the most appropriate stone to assist you.

Amazonite – The Soothing Stone: This stone is known for its powerful ability to calm and soothe the wearer. It relaxes the body, mind, and emotions, so it's good for reducing stress and anxiety. Amazonite balances male and female energies and encourages understanding and harmony in relationships. It allows you to consider a problem from a more objective space.

Bloodstone – Stone of Courage: This is an intense healing stone. It inspires great courage and helps you maneuver through change and to accept that the upset of turmoil can bring great rewards. It is incredibly grounding and protective.

Emerald – Stone of the Heart: This gemstone strengthens relationships, increases patience, and encourages living a life of integrity. This stone prevents negative emotions from festering and allows you to bring more compassion into your life. It helps you strengthen all of the relationships in your life and connect to family traditions.

Green Aventurine – Stone of Heart Healing: Aventurine is a very effective "heart healer" and creates a safe healing space during heartache. This gemstone balances and restores all energies within the body—chakras, masculine and feminine, yin yang energies, and more, to help with healing and wellness. This stone protects from energetic attachments and is useful in harsh environments. The green variety of aventurine, in particular, is a stone that attracts abundance and growth, allowing more happiness, love, and relationships into your life.

Green Calcite – Stone of Renewal: All Calcite is a powerful cleanser and amplifier of energy. Green Calcite is a powerful mental and energetic healer. It dissolves attachment to outdated, rigid beliefs that no longer support you. It supports you as you let go of the familiar and adopt healthier habits and thought patterns.

Green Tourmaline (Verdelite) – Stone of Healing and Balance: This crystal boosts healing energies. It stimulates all areas of the heart, such as compassion, tenderness, and patience. This is a nurturing stone that instills a sense of belonging and peace. It aids in relaxation and sleep to allow healing processes to thrive.

Jade – Stone of Manifestation: Jade is known to attract luck and prosperity. This helps with the dreamers and visionaries in the world. Jade helps you realize your potential and purpose in life. It gives you the confidence and self-assuredness to bring your dreams into reality. Jade helps to assure success in your endeavors. It helps you to remember and process dreams.

Malachite – Stone of Transformation: Assists you during changing situations and provides for the transfer of sacred information leading to spiritual evolution. It also protects you during these times of change. It helps with scenarios of rebirth and releasing negativity from the change.

Moldavite – Stone of Universal Compassion: A tektite is formed when a meteor strikes the Earth and melts with the elements at the location. This is an incredibly high vibrational and uplifting crystal. It is connected with the breadth of the universe and is said to help us channel information from all of the universe. Moldavite is especially helpful for people who find the suffering and tragedies of human life too much to bear. It enables you to send out love, compassion, and healing to all others in the world, rather than taking on all of their pain.

Peridot – Stone of Cleansing: This gemstone is a powerful overall cleanser. It cleanses the aura, energy, and chakras. It helps you release your burdens and guilt to forgive yourself. Peridot helps to release old habits and behavior patterns to make room for more productive and healthy patterns. Helps to dissolve jealousy, bitterness, anger, and spite.

Seraphinite – Stone of the Angels: Is often referred to for its higher energies and relationship with angels. It is said to help contact angels and communicate with them. Psychically, Seraphinite is beneficial for intuition and psychic awareness. This stone can be very protective of the heart chakra and is helpful for sending unconditional love. This is a purifying stone that helps you find your higher purpose and will.

Serpentine – Stone of the Earth: This gemstone has a deep connection with the spirit and energy of the Earth. It helps you to feel more grounded and in control of life. It supports deep meditation and connection with kundalini energy straight to the core of the planet. It helps to awaken intuitive and psychic abilities and clears the chakras.

Tree and Moss Agate – Stone of Plentitude: This stone attracts abundance in all areas of your life. It can be used to help nourish and heal plants. It creates a peaceful environment and helps you truly enjoy the present moment. Tree Agate is a soothing, grounding gemstone that helps you remain calm and centered during crisis situations.

GEMSTONE MEDITATION FOR HEALING

This is a guided meditation designed specifically to promote a healing energy using green gemstones. If you are in need of healing and compassion, then identify a green gemstone and try this crystal meditation. Go at your own pace, as you feel comfortable. The more familiar you are with the energy of your gemstone, the less time you may need to meditate to attain the benefits.

1. First, locate a green gemstone to use during this meditation.
2. Find a comfortable place to sit. You can sit on a cushion on the floor, a chair, or directly on the ground outside. Make sure you can sit tall and comfortably for about ten to twenty minutes.
3. Hold the green gemstone in your nondominant hand. This is your receiving hand that will take in the energy of the crystal.
4. Close your eyes and begin to take slow deep breaths.
5. Bring your awareness to where your legs and sitting bones are touching the floor or ground. Take a moment to feel

the seat underneath you. You are completely supported and protected by the entire Earth underneath you.

6. Bring your attention to your body and take note of how your body, mind, emotions, and energy feel right now. Don't try to fix, change, or judge any experience. Just take note. Be IN your body and see how it feels.

7. Now take a minute to feel the stone in your hand. Take note of its weight, smoothness, texture, and how it feels as you hold it.

8. Pull your shoulders back a little to open your heart area.

9. Imagine you are sitting in a lush, green forest surrounded by green grass, plants, and trees.

10. Bring to mind whatever is causing you discomfort or suffering.

11. As you inhale, imagine you are breathing in the vibrant, healing energy of the green plants.

12. Imagine that the energy of the green Earth and gemstone are bringing peace and balance to this situation, whether your source of imbalance is an injury, illness, relationship, or frustration. The green energy you are taking in is bringing peace.

13. Then as you exhale, release whatever it is that is causing imbalance and suffering down into the Earth. Continue this cycle of breathing for a few minutes.

14. Imagine yourself as whole, strong, and renewed.

15. Then, take a moment to send out compassion to all others who have also suffered as you have.

16. After a few minutes, bring your awareness back to your breath and body. How does your body, mind, emotions, or energy feel now? Has anything changed since the beginning of the meditation? Don't try to force anything. It may take several meditation sessions to notice real change, but take note of anything. Journaling is especially helpful during this process.
17. Then release the imagery and come back to your breath. Just breathe and feel the seat underneath you.
18. Take a few final deep breaths.
19. When you feel ready, open your eyes.
20. Take a few minutes to journal about your experience.

PINK | LOVE

CHAPTER 14

PINK GEMSTONES | LOVE

THE SECOND COLOR that influences the heart chakra is pink. It is a warm, friendly color. Pink is a color that represents a deep, all-encompassing love. Gentler than red, it exudes the warmth of love rather than the passion. The pink color of the heart represents caring and empathy. Pink wraps us in a blanket of community support and appreciation.

Pink flowers symbolize friendship and appreciation and are a great was to say "thank you" to someone. Wearing pink can lift our mood, inspire hope, and calm intense feelings. Surrounding yourself with light pinks can foster a nurturing and soothing environment. Hot and dark pinks will enable you to stand out and make a statement. The many shades of pink can influence us in countless ways, but they all lead straight to the heart.

An attraction to pink crystals indicates that you are in search of some form of love. It is more complex than wanting a romantic partner. There are so many levels and flavors of love that we can seek. Our heart has many facets, like an expertly fashioned gemstone. Pink helps us identify which facet needs attention and how we can bring loving care to that aspect of our heart. Working with pink gemstones enables us to expand our capacity for love, self-compassion, and forgiveness.

Pink Gemstones Help You Cultivate More . . .

Unconditional Love

The influences of love in our lives are vast and varied. From the moment we are born we seek the loving, comforting touch of our parents. As youth we yearn for the love and admiration of friends. As we get older, we open ourselves up to the love of a companion. We then may go on to become parents and love our own children. Love flavors every time period of our lives. However, the opportunity for heartache is also possible, and many would say inevitable, from the very start of life as well.

Our capacity to love contributes to our overall well-being. If you are able to willingly give love to those around you, and receive love in return, then your life is full of comfort, support, and appreciation.

Our hearts are very tender though and even small wounds leave large scars. We may unknowingly build walls around the heart to avoid being hurt again. We may start to believe that we are not worthy of love, or we may feel foolish expressing love if it has been rejected in the past. Pink gemstones help us identify where these heart wounds live, how we may be blocking the reception of love, and help us feel secure enough to be vulnerable to the experience of love.

Rose Quartz is a powerful gemstone of the heart. Meditating with Rose Quartz can allow you to open up your heart space, be willing to receive love, dissolve barriers you may have erected to avoid love, and help you send love out to the world.

If you find that you just can't seem to find the right partner, or the relationships are short-lived, then you may be sabotaging your own desires. Pink crystals will help you notice the subtle ways you may be rejecting the love you are searching for. A perfect example of this is from the movie *So I Married an Axe Murderer* when Mike Myers' character explains why he broke up with his latest girlfriend.

"She smelled like soup." Are you looking for reasons to protect your heart? Pink gemstones will help you release your armor and find fulfilling, genuine love.

Self-Acceptance

The love we feel isn't just directed toward other people. It is vital that we be able to love ourselves just as much. Being able to love yourself is the foundation for loving relationships with others. If you continually feel you are not worthy of love, then you will have nothing available for your relationships. It is like a cup of liquid. Until you are able to fill it to the top, there won't be any to spill over for another.

Pink is a color that fosters self-love, self-compassion, self-appreciation, and self-care. We can be our own harshest critics and don't often treat ourselves the way we would a cherished friend. This is an issue that requires focused and immediate attention. You should act toward yourself as you would a friend. Rather than berate yourself when you don't succeed, how would your best friend act toward you? They may tell you that it's okay, you still did great and should try again! They would give you a hug and bring you treats when you feel low.

Pink gemstones foster this sense of friendship toward yourself. They are nurturing when you don't feel capable of loving yourself, or when you feel unloved by others. If you find yourself under the attack of your self-critic, find a pink crystal such as Rose Quartz, hold it in your receiving hand, kick the judgmental inner voice out the door, and give yourself some encouragement. Feel appreciation for yourself just as you are, commend yourself for trying, and know that you are a beautiful soul deserving of immense love.

Forgiveness

Heart wounds can run very deep and exist for years. The emotions and symptoms of heartache and betrayal can have a firm grip on our heart, mind, and energy. It can feel so very hard to forgive after we've received injury to the heart core. Luckily, pink can support us and helps us detach from negative emotions such as anger and bitterness. These feelings could be directed at someone else, but they can also be aimed at ourselves. You could be hurt at your partner for the harsh breakup, or you could just as easily be blaming yourself. Whichever way your pain is pointed, pink gemstones can ease the rays of hurt and blame.

Hold a pink gemstone in your sending hand if you want to send forgiveness to someone else. When you hold on to bitterness and anger toward another person, it only hurts yourself. They are not affected in the slightest. As you hold the pink gemstone, allow yourself to release the grip of suffering. Rhodonite is useful for this practice. Know that you can move forward without giving any more of your energy away to that person. You have so many opportunities for friendships and loving relationships ahead of you.

On the other hand, we could blame ourselves for the outcome of a failed relationship, a fight with a friend, or a misunderstanding with a partner. Even well after the event, you may still feel responsible and beat yourself up with guilt. This is unhealthy and blocks our ability to love ourselves and to enter into new relationships. If you are having a difficult time having forgiveness for yourself, working with Mangano Calcite is especially useful. Hold this crystal in your receiving hand to invite self-forgiveness. Remind yourself of the valuable lessons you've learned from the experience and know that you are still lovable and deserving of love.

Signs You Need More PINK Gemstone Energy

Try to incorporate pink gemstones into your daily Crystal Wisdom practice if you are experiencing the following symptoms or occurrences in your life.

- Seeking more love in your life
- Looking for a dedicated partner
- Finding it difficult to commit to a relationship
- Feeling uncomfortable expressing your love to others
- Lacking trust with romantic partners
- Having a challenging relationship with a friend or family member
- Feeling especially self-critical and judgmental of yourself
- Resisting appreciating yourself just as you are
- Finding it hard to forgive yourself or someone else
- Feeling deep guilt or shame
- Blaming yourself for relationship failures
- Feeling you don't deserve love

PINK GEMSTONES FOR LOVE

These pink stones increase your opportunities for love in your life but also provide the unique supportive benefits listed below. Study these additional healing properties to help you identify the most appropriate stone to assist you.

Kunzite – Stone of Spirituality and Protection: Kunzite is an incredibly peaceful and open-hearted gemstone. It helps you sink deep into meditation, opens the heart center to expansive compassion, and helps you find peace and connection to all. It is also very protective and strengthens the energetic field. It creates a shield around the aura that repels negativity, unwanted attachments, and dark influences.

Mangano Calcite – Stone of Forgiveness: This stone helps you to release the fear and grief that paralyzes the heart. Mangano is an excellent aid to help you recover from trauma and assault. It prevents nightmares and increases self-acceptance. This is a stone of the Angelic realm and reminds you that you are never alone.

Morganite (Pink Beryl) – Stone of Heart Expansion: This crystal helps you attract love and maintain it. It encourages healthy boundaries and the regular nurturing of a loving relationship. It also allows you to recognize the negative and limiting emotions that block spiritual development. Morganite eases unexpressed feelings and brings ignored emotional needs to the surface for acknowledgment and resolution. It helps you to see where you might be unconsciously preventing healing.

Pink Calcite – Stone of Compassion: This crystal helps you develop deep, unwavering compassion for both yourself and others. It helps you overcome self-criticism and self-blame. This stone connects to the loving energy of Quan Yin and helps us cultivate unconditional love for all.

Pink Tourmaline – Stone of Trust: This crystal helps you trust in the power of love. It helps you navigate change with love and compassion. Pink Tourmaline is a powerful magnet for attracting love in your life but reminds you that you need to love yourself first before you can open the door to receiving love from others.

Rhodochrosite – Stone of Love: This stone radiates the strongest power in the universe, the power of love. It balances and restores feelings of love and helps heal the wounds of love. It fosters love for all aspects of yourself and others.

Rhodonite – Stone of Enduring Love: Rhodonite energizes the heart chakra and brings the vibration of unconditional love to the physical plane. It is known as the "first aid stone" as it helps people in the midst of crisis, trauma, and shock. This stone helps you remember why you love someone even if the relationship is strained. Rhodonite also inspires empathy and to see the other side of the picture.

Rose Quartz – Stone of Unconditional Love: It opens the heart chakra to all forms of love: self-love, family love, platonic love, and romantic love. Rose quartz has excellent protection energies during pregnancy and childbirth. It also brings gentleness, forgiveness, and tolerance. It inspires deep self-love and acceptance.

Strawberry Quartz – Stone of Pure Joy: This stone helps you to bring immense joy, love, and humor in your life. It helps to create a joyful, peaceful home if placed in your living environment. You can bring divine love to everything you do. Strawberry Quartz helps you to release restrictions you have imposed on yourself and live with more freedom.

Thulite – Stone of Enjoyment: Thulite allows you to open your heart to experience the pure joy of life. It allows you to balance the aspects of logic and love, helping to integrate the heart and mind. It helps you recognize the divine nature of all people, creatures, and nature. It enhances relationships, attracts new friends, and boosts social confidence.

GEMSTONE MEDITATION FOR LOVE

This is a guided meditation designed specifically to promote a loving energy, using pink gemstones. If you wish to expand your capacity to love, then identify a pink gemstone and try this crystal meditation. Go at your own pace, as you feel comfortable. The more familiar you are with the energy of your gemstone, the less time you may need to meditate to attain the benefits.

1. First, locate a pink gemstone to use during this meditation.
2. Find a comfortable place to sit. You can sit on a cushion on the floor, a chair, or directly on the ground outside. Make sure you can sit tall and comfortably for about ten to twenty minutes.
3. Hold the pink gemstone in your nondominant hand. This is your receiving hand that will take in the energy of the crystal.
4. Close your eyes and begin to take slow deep breaths.
5. Bring your awareness to where your legs and sitting bones are touching the floor or ground. Take a moment to feel the seat underneath you. You are completely supported and protected by the entire Earth underneath you.
6. Bring your attention to your body and take note of how your body, mind, emotions, and energy feel right now. Don't try to fix, change, or judge any experience, just take note. Be IN your body and see how it feels.
7. Now take a minute to feel the stone in your hand. Take note of its weight, smoothness, texture, and how it feels as you hold it.

8. Pull your shoulders back a little to open your heart area.
9. Imagine a beautiful pink flower blooming open at your heart center.
10. It radiates a soft pink energy all around you.
11. As you inhale feel your body filling with an immense sensation of love. Love for everyone, for yourself, for your loved ones, for the population of the world. Allow this feeling to flood your body for a few minutes.
12. Then as you exhale, picture any walls, barriers, or shields you may have around you just dissolving and floating away on your breath.
13. Feel the sensation of having this uninhibited and unobstructed capability for giving and receiving love.
14. As you breathe in, fill with love for yourself. As you exhale, send it out to anyone you choose, or everyone on the planet. Experience this cycle of love, breathing for a few minutes.
15. After a few minutes, bring your awareness back to your breath and body. How do your body, mind, emotions, or energy feel now? Has anything changed since the beginning of the meditation? Don't try to force anything. It may take several meditation sessions to notice real change, but take note of anything. Journaling is especially helpful during this process.
16. Then release the imagery and come back to your breath. Just breathe and feel the seat underneath you.
17. Take a few final deep breaths.
18. When you feel ready, open your eyes.
19. Take a few minutes to journal about your experience.

BLUE | AUTHENTICITY

CHAPTER 15

BLUE GEMSTONES | AUTHENTICITY

IN THIS BOOK I WILL BE DISCUSSING TWO SHADES, or intensities, of blue. Both shades elicit different emotions and reactions within the body, heart, and spirit and I felt they each deserved a dedicated exploration. This chapter is focused on the darker shades of blue. These shades are commonly called dark blue, royal blue, or navy blue.

This is the blue of blueberries, denim, the deep ocean, and the night sky. Like the vast ocean, blue invites us deep within ourselves. To sit in quiet stillness to explore our very being. There is a stillness to all shades of blue that is comforting and soothing. Blue is the most prevalent color on the planet, so we feel at home and comforted with blue.

Blue is associated with the throat chakra and our ability for expression and communication. It helps us tap into our deepest self and offer our soul to the world. Working with blue gemstones will open access to your personal truth, the courage to allow that truth to shine brightly, and the ability to express your truth in the most effective way possible.

Blue Gemstones Help You Cultivate More...

Truth
The throat chakra and the color blue invite us on a journey into our inner world. All of the previous chakras focused on the relationship

with our exterior world. As we venture higher in the chakra system we delve into our inner and spiritual development.

The deep blue night sky invites us into the mystery of our inner self. It encourages introspection and self-contemplation. It supports our ability to look at the mystery within and to open the pages of the great book containing our inner knowledge. In my book, *Crystal Wisdom*, I discuss in depth about connecting to your Inner Guide. This space of blue is where you can begin that relationship. You can start tapping into the truth that you already hold within. We already know the answers to our deepest questions, the solutions to our challenges, the healthiest choices, and the most nourishing actions for our spiritual evolution.

Sitting with blue gemstones helps us settle into the quiet space of meditation. It is with meditation that we can shift our view from the external occurrences surrounding us into the experience of our pure being. Disconnect from the swirling thoughts of the day and tap into the voice within. If you have a question, sit with a blue gemstone like Apatite, and ask yourself. Give the "thinking mind" a break and resist the urge to "figure it out." Allow the soft voice of your Inner Guide to provide you with the answers you already know. Notice how it feels when that answer arises. That answer should resonate and feel true.

Use this process to delve the depths of what you believe and feel is your personal truth. Disconnect from the influence of others' opinions, social media, and the bias of the news. Discover how you genuinely and truly feel about the important facets of life. As you get more familiar with the feeling of your inner wisdom, you will start to learn what the felt sense of truth is within you and it can be a powerful guiding system.

Authenticity

It is this access to vast, deep truth that enables us to uncover our personal authenticity. Many of us feel that we don't know what we stand for, are unsure of our direction in life, or may feel a general dissatisfaction for how we maneuver in life. Many people are often pressured to conform to other's ideas of how to act, dress, work, or express themselves. This feels false and the mask of conformity is uncomfortable. It leaves us feeling ungrounded, adrift, and in search of something more meaningful.

The search for personal authenticity can be a life-long pursuit, but the sooner we can step into that space of truth in our lives, the more fulfilling and expansive the rest of our life journey can be. Many people feel lost, dissatisfied, and adrift but don't know why and don't know how to resolve it. The answers to the intensely personal struggle can all be found within.

On one hand, you may already know what is true for you. You may dream and wish for a day in which you can live the genuine, authentic way you desire, but you may be blocked by fear. Blue gemstones help you acknowledge the importance of living an authentic life and they inspire the courage to share your true self with others. The color blue helps to bridge our inner and outer worlds. To present what is beautiful and true to the outside world. Meditate with a blue gemstone, such as Sodalite, to recognize the power of authentic living and to build the courage to be yourself.

On the other hand, maybe you don't already know how your true self wants to live, but you feel that aching dissatisfaction of living by others' expectations. You know you don't want to be a teacher like your mother hopes you will be, but you don't know what your soul desires as a profession. Meditating with Lapis Lazuli will help your true interests, passions, and life goals to arise. Experience how it feels to tap into the discovery of an aspect of your true self and the intense fulfillment that you feel when you live by that truth. You will experience the power of an authentic life.

I have found that when we connect our authentic feelings and personalities into our everyday activities, they become richer and much more satisfying, even if we already enjoyed them before. It brings a new feeling of passion to your job, hobbies, relationships, and creative efforts. If you want to experience the magic of authentic living, then incorporate more blue gemstones into your reflective and meditation practices.

Communication

The throat chakra primarily regulates our ability to communicate. This becomes the other side of the bridge between inner and outer worlds, when we express our thoughts, ideas, and creations to others. If your words and intent are fed by your inner truth, then you begin to manifest truth in your life.

The color blue guides us to inspire others and to share knowledge and wisdom. Blue helps you formulate the most effective words for your message. It inspires confidence in your ideas and the courage to share your words to other people. Keep a blue gemstone near you as you are composing any form of communication. This could include emails, Powerpoint presentations, a speech, a course manual, a book, or even crafting your message before going into a meeting. If you are struggling with how to express an idea, blue crystals can assist by disconnecting you from the "figure it out" brain and into your uninhibited true feelings.

Wear this stone if you have to give a presentation, speech, or enter a negotiation. It is especially helpful if you are afraid of public speaking. It inspires confidence in your words, voice, and speech. Blue gemstones are very effective for managers, leaders, and liaisons.

Blue can help you share your vision with a team, share expertise, and guidance. Blue gems can strengthen rapport with your audience and an enthusiasm for your message.

Finally, blue gemstones are especially useful if you need to have a difficult conversation. When unveiling your true, authentic self to others, this may involve sharing some truth that may be uncomfortable for the person you are talking to. You may also feel fear about revealing your truth and that is okay, because stones like Blue Aventurine provide inner strength and courage for those discussions. Your true self wants to be free, and you *will* feel better even as you share your truth. Managers and leaders also benefit from the color blue because it will help them develop the most compassionate words for difficult conversations and announcements.

The color blue helps us bring the deep mystery of our inner soul into the bright light of day. Blue enables us to let our radiant authentic self shine brightly, and it helps us take the first step on the path to a truly enriching soulful life journey. Blue gemstones cultivate a presence and message of sincerity and honesty both toward yourself and toward other people.

Signs You Need More BLUE Gemstone Energy

Try to incorporate blue gemstones into your daily Crystal Wisdom practice if you are experiencing the following symptoms or occurrences in your life.

- Fear of expressing your opinions
- Hiding an aspect of yourself from others
- A desire to explore your inner truth
- Difficulty connecting to your Inner Guide
- Have an upcoming difficult conversation with someone

- Find yourself at a loss for words
- Crafting any form of communication
- Speaking to a group of people
- Fear of public speaking
- Are in leadership or a managerial position
- Are a liaison between people or groups
- Are a writer, editor, or lyricist

BLUE GEMSTONES FOR AUTHENTICITY

These blue stones encourage you to lead an honest and authentic life, but also provide the unique supportive benefits listed below. Study these additional healing properties to help you identify the most appropriate stone to assist you.

Apatite – Stone of Insight: When used with spiritual practice, Apatite can be used to develop deeper states of meditation, reflection, inner wisdom, intuitive insights, peace and oneness with humanity. It helps to address blocks, sluggishness, or over activity of the chakras—it brings them into balance. Apatite speeds the effects of other stones and therapies. Helps to increase your sense of service and development of humanitarian efforts.

Azurite – Stone of Heaven: Azurite encourages the pursuit of spiritual goals, divine communication, and awakening psychic abilities. It enhances the flow of information from the universe. Azurite also calms a troubled mind, allowing you to release worries and doubts about your destiny.

Blue Aventurine – Stone of Inner Strength: This is a stone that encourages self-discipline, responsibility, and inner strength. It helps you feel "more comfortable in your own skin." It helps those who have been avoiding the pressures of adulthood. This stone helps to awaken intuitive and psychic abilities.

Blue Tourmaline (Indicolite) – Stone of Awakening and Healing: Blue Tourmaline helps to awaken intuitive abilities and clarify your Highest Good. It encourages you to be of service to others, expand compassion, and develop a love of compassionate truth. This stone supports healers and prevents negativity from sticking to the healer. This gem enables repressed feelings to arise to the surface for healing.

Dumortierite – Stone of Expression: This stone helps with all forms of communication and personal expression. It will help you realize your personal vision and speak your truth. Dumortierite will also give you the courage to assert your true potential and help you vocalize your talents to others. "To sell yourself."

Hawk's Eye – Stone of Communication: Blue Tigers Eye, which is also known as Hawks Eye, enhances integrity of communication and practical communication. It can help you find the courage to recognize thoughts and ideas, and the willpower to carry them into the physical realm. Blue Tiger's Eye can be used for protection, especially of the upper chakras. It is also said to bring good luck to one who wears or carries it.

Lapis Lazuli – Stone of Total Awareness: Lapis is said to have existed "before time existed" and helps you access ancient knowledge. It helps to expand awareness and intellectual capacity allowing you to easily attune with the intuitive and psychic aspects of your nature. Lapis helps you think rationally about subjective topics, so you can translate vision into real life. As a throat chakra stone, it helps you see and speak the truth and to discover your most authentic true self.

Pietersite – **Stone of Spirituality:** Pietersite has been said to contain the "keys to the kingdom of heaven" by linking the spiritual realm with everyday living. It reminds you that you are first a spiritual being experiencing the human condition, not the other way around. This stone helps to dispel illusion and assist one in the recognition of the beauty of the soul.

Sodalite – **Stone of True Voice:** Calms the mind, eliminates confusion, and stimulates the intellect. It also enhances truthfulness in emotions, allowing one to speak honestly from the heart. This stone supports your efforts to speak authentically and own your true voice. If you feel you have been hiding an aspect of yourself, Sodalite encourages you to be open and honest about it. It fosters solidarity in groups and helps move to common goals.

Sapphire – **Stone of Wisdom:** All sapphire helps you seek and attain deep wisdom. Each color has its own primary source. Blue Sapphire supports you as you seek spiritual wisdom and enables you to share this truth with others. Blue sapphire transmutes negative energies.

GEMSTONE MEDITATION FOR AUTHENTICITY

This is a guided meditation designed specifically to tap into your inner truth using blue gemstones. If you are in need of the truth and wisdom to craft a message, then identify a blue gemstone and try this crystal meditation. Go at your own pace, as you feel comfortable. The more familiar you are with the energy of your gemstone, the less time you may need to meditate to attain the benefits.

1. First, locate a blue gemstone to use during this meditation.
2. Find a comfortable place to sit. You can sit on a cushion on the floor, a chair, or directly on the ground outside. Make sure you can sit tall and comfortably for about ten to twenty minutes.
3. Hold the blue gemstone in your nondominant hand. This is your receiving hand that will take in the energy of the crystal.
4. Close your eyes and begin to take slow deep breaths.
5. Bring your awareness to where your legs and sitting bones are touching the floor or ground. Take a moment to feel the seat underneath you. You are completely supported and protected by the entire Earth underneath you.
6. Bring your attention to your body and take note of how your body, mind, emotions, and energy feel right now. Don't try to fix, change, or judge any experience, just take note. Be IN your body and see how it feels.
7. Now take a minute to feel the stone in your hand. Take note of its weight, smoothness, texture, and how it feels as you hold it.
8. Lift your chin just a little to open up your throat area.
9. As you inhale, imagine your throat area filling with nourishing energy. Take several deep breaths like this.
10. Allow your awareness to sink lower and deeper into your body.

11. Release your "thinking mind" and just breathe. Bring to mind the message you need to consider.
12. What is the primary message you need to convey? Notice if there is fear associated with this conversation.
13. Ask your Inner Guide for the most effective yet compassionate way to word your message. Wait a few minutes for this to arise.
14. Ask Your Inner Guide for the confidence and skill to express yourself. As you inhale, you are filling yourself with the confidence inherent in the truth of your message. As you exhale, release the fear out with your breath.
15. Continue this breathing cycle until the hold of fear has dissolved.
16. After a few minutes, bring your awareness back to your breath and body. How do your body, mind, emotions, or energy feel now? Has anything changed since the beginning of the meditation? Don't try to force anything. It may take several meditation sessions to notice real change, but take note of anything. Journaling is especially helpful during this process.
17. Then release the imagery and come back to your breath. Just breathe and feel the seat underneath you.
18. Take a few final deep breaths.
19. When you feel ready, open your eyes.
20. Take a few minutes to journal about your experience.

LIGHT BLUE
SPIRITUAL EXPANSION

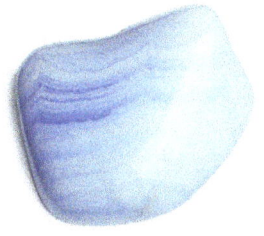

CHAPTER 16

LIGHT BLUE GEMSTONES
SPIRITUAL EXPANSION

THIS CHAPTER FOCUSES ON THE LIGHTER SHADES OF BLUE, such as pale blue, sky blue, robin's nest blue, and turquoise. The energy of this color is distinctive from its darker blue range. Dark blue invites us deep within, while light blue opens the doors and welcomes us outside. This energetic bridge is vital in cultivating a steady, grounded spiritual practice. It enables us to be in the present moment, while still expanding our spiritual awareness. Blue illuminates the beginnings of one's spiritual path.

All shades of blue resonate with the throat chakra. The element of the throat chakra is ether which represents space. The space within us, surrounding us, and throughout the universe. Space is limitless and unbounded. Light blue cultivates this energy of space, the vastness, the breadth, and the unfettered feeling of wide-open distance.

Working with blue gemstones feels like a bird taking flight. They can help us expand our awareness past the bounds of our physical body, enabling us to take flight and be free of those parts of life that are constricting, and are extremely supportive when developing a connection with our spiritual world.

Light Blue Gemstones Help You Cultivate More . . .

Expansion

As mentioned before, blue is the most prevalent color on the planet. It is the color of the oceans and the sky, so it inspires a feeling of vastness and great expanse. Light blue rouses a sense of openness that is expansive like a cloudless blue sky. Have you ever looked up at a perfectly blue sky and felt the magnitude of the open sky? This is a reminder that we, too, are as expansive as the sky. We are much more than a physical body. We are energy, spirit, and part of the collective energy of the universe.

Sitting with light blue gemstones can help you explore the space outside of your body. They assist you in getting in touch with your aura and energetic body. Blue stones, such as Larimar, help you feel that your energy is not just a little light within you, but shines well outside the bounds of your body. Meditate with a light blue stone to help you feel the vastness of your energy self. It helps you sense the breadth of your aura and get familiar with working with all of your energy sources rather than just relying on physical energy alone.

Freedom

Light blue gemstones inspire a sense of great freedom and independence. Both intensities of blue work hand-in-hand to create personal freedom. After working with deeper blue, you are no longer weighted by the expectations of others because you trust in your inner self. You can feel free and confident in living an independent life carved out by your connection with inner truth. With the support of light blue, you are inspired to explore a life with a vast amount of options. As the phrase states, "The sky is the limit." This is how it feels when you no longer live life to please others and seek to nourish your own soul with authentic choices.

Light blue often helps when I am feeling inundated by the heavy responsibilities of being an adult. I lie down on the ground outside, with a light blue gem, and look up at the sky. Blue Lace Agate is extremely potent for me. I can feel my burdens melting down into the ground beneath me and am uplifted by the lightness of the light blue sky. It helps to remind me that the heaviness I feel is self-imposed and I can free myself of the mental stress whenever I feel too strained. Responsibilities are not a weight chain, but a chance to serve others and craft a satisfying life.

Light blue is extremely supportive when you feel confined or trapped within your physical body. Many people associate the existence of their being with their body. This attachment can cause great fear and distress when anything happens to the body. If you feel afraid of injuries to your body or fear the death of your physical body, sit with Aquamarine to release attachment to your physical body. If this is an attachment you identify with, meditations that help you reduce the sensation of the physical body can remind you that you are so much more than a body of skin and bones. Your spirit, soul, and energy are just as much a part of your human experience as your body. Some will argue even more so if you believe the spirit and soul live on after death. Developing a relationship with your spirit and energetic self will free you of the grasping clinging to your physical existence.

For this very reason, light blue crystals are useful for those in hospice care to help them release attachment to the physical body. If you work in a hospice, or have a loved one in hospice care, carrying a light blue gem with you will help you support their end-of-life experience. If they are afraid, you will be able to gently reassure them and remind them that the end of the body is not the end of everything. There are even meditations designed to help release the spirit from the body at the moment of death. One such meditation is the

Buddhist practice of Phowa. This is a common practice that allows a person to practice letting go of the physical body and transitioning into the peace of the next phase of existence.

Connection to Spirit

As we move upward from the heart chakra, we begin the journey of getting to know our spiritual self. This path begins with the dark blue connection to our inner world and continues with light blue as we open up to the spirit world. Not only can you experience the expansive freedom of your energetic body, but you can connect with higher guides that provide support and guidance throughout our lives.

If you have sought a deeper connection with spirit and angel guides, light blue will help you open up to receive their wisdom. Higher guides might also include your higher self, the universe, animal spirits, and whatever greater entity you feel looks out for your spiritual well-being. Stones such as Angelite and Celestite will aid you in initiating and strengthening your connection to your guides. They will enable you to feel their presence, ask for guidance, recognize the message they offer you, and feel confident in applying the wisdom.

Working with light blue gemstones, like K2 Stone, are extremely supportive when starting spiritual practice. If you are starting to learn meditation, energy work, or spiritual and religious classes, bring a light blue stone with you to help you be receptive to these new experiences. They will encourage a willingness and confidence to explore the non-physical aspects of your life.

Signs You Need More LIGHT BLUE Gemstone Energy

Try to incorporate light blue gemstones into your daily Crystal Wisdom practice if you are experiencing the following symptoms or occurrences in your life.

1. Welcoming a connection with your spirit or angel guides
2. Are seeking guidance from a higher source
3. Feeling confined within your physical body
4. Feeling housebound due to the weather
5. Wanting to explore the area of your energetic body
6. Exploring out-of-body experiences, such as astral projection and dream journeying
7. Focusing on expansive meditations
8. Are in hospice care or have a loved one in hospice
9. Practicing end-of-life meditations, such as the Buddhist Phowa practice

BLUE GEMSTONES FOR SPIRITUAL EXPANSION

These light blue stones help open your soul to receive light and guidance from the universe, but also provide the unique supportive benefits listed below. Study these additional healing properties to help you identify the most appropriate stone to assist you.

Angelite – Stone of Awareness: Raises the state of conscious awareness. Angelite facilitates contact with your angels and spirit guides and helps to connect with your higher self. Because of its ability to deepen attunement and heighten perception, Angelite is a powerful stone for healers. It also provides protection for the environment or the body.

Aquamarine – Stone of Courage: This stone has often been used for protection on journeys, especially for those who travel on water. Helps stabilize and harmonize unsettled surroundings. It soothes and calms frayed nerves and helps reduce fears. This stone gives you the courage to bring issues to closure and to release what you no longer need.

Blue Calcite – Stone of Comfort: All Calcite is a powerful cleanser and amplifier of energy. Blue Calcite is one of the most soothing, comforting stones there is. It protects those who are empathic from taking on the entire energy of a room. This crystal creates a shield of cleansing light around your aura and allows you to release the body for astral travel.

Blue Lace Agate – Stone of Expansion: Can help the wearer reach extremely high spiritual spaces. It contains the qualities of flight, air, movement, and grace. It is highly cooling and calming and brings peace into life. It is a highly inspirational influence when used for inner attunement.

Blue Topaz – Stone of Inner Wisdom: This gemstone connects you deeply with your angel and spirit guides. It enables you to look within and recognize your own inner truth and wisdom. It helps to deepen meditation and to live life guided by your spiritual aspirations.

Celestite – Stone of Information: It helps with accessing information from the angelic realm, helps clear and balance the chakras, and allows you to recall your gifts from the divine. It is also excellent for working with mental and intelligence-based projects.

Hemimorphite – Stone of Spiritual Development: This is a very high vibrational stone that raises the vibration of the wearer. It encourages rapid personal and spiritual development. It helps you acknowledge your responsibility for raising the vibration of others, while still maintaining your own spiritual practice. This stone protects you from manipulation by others.

Kyanite – Stone of Cleansing: This is one stone that never needs clearing or cleansing! It will not accumulate negative energies. It aligns all chakras immediately and balances the energies of mind, body, heart, and spirit. It supports deep and steady meditation.

Larimar – Stone of Spirituality: The blue color of the Larimar reflects the "sea" of all consciousness, which gives freedom from self-imposed limitations and a sense of peace in finding the truth. This stone helps to dissolve any blockages restricting your journey to spiritual awakening. It is a stone of the sea and Earth and helps with Earth healing practices. This is a stone of gentle love and peace and helps to find soul mates. Larimar is good for calming and balancing excess energies.

Trolleite – Stone of Awakening: Trolleite is an amazingly high vibration stone that connects you deeply with your spirit and angel guides and encourages full awakening. It helps to deepen meditation and connects you to your deep cellular memories from previous existences. This supports our access to inner wisdom and helps determine why you feel and react the way you do to situations in the current life. This stone is a powerful manifestation stone, so it is useful during moon rituals, vision rituals, and bringing your dreams to reality!

Turquoise - Stone of Purification: Often used in ancient amulets, Turquoise is a wonderful healing stone. It channels the healing energy of the Earth Mother to cleanse and balance the energetic body. It enhances intuition and communication with the spirit realm. It works extremely well to guard against exhaustion, depression, and panic attacks.

GEMSTONE MEDITATION FOR SPIRITUAL EXPANSION

This is a guided meditation designed specifically for promoting a sense of expansion beyond the body using light blue gemstones. If you desire a connection with Spirit, then identify a light blue gemstone and try this crystal meditation. Go at your own pace, as you feel comfortable. The more familiar you are with the energy of your gemstone, the less time you may need to meditate to attain the benefits.

1. First, locate a light blue gemstone to use during this meditation.

2. Find a comfortable place to sit. You can sit on a cushion on the floor, a chair, or directly on the ground outside. Make sure you can sit tall and comfortably for about ten to twenty minutes.

3. Hold the light blue gemstone in your nondominant hand. This is your receiving hand that will take in the energy of the crystal.

4. Close your eyes and begin to take slow deep breaths.

5. Bring your awareness to where your legs and sitting bones are touching the floor or ground. Take a moment to feel the seat underneath you. You are completely supported and protected by the entire Earth underneath you.

6. Bring your attention to your body and take note of how your body, mind, emotions, and energy feel right now.

Don't try to fix, change, or judge any experience, just take note. Be IN your body and see how it feels.

7. Now take a minute to feel the stone in your hand. Take note of its weight, smoothness, texture, and how it feels as you hold it.

8. Lift your chin a bit to open and expand your throat area.

9. As you inhale, imagine your body filling with bright light.

10. When your body is full of light, begin to allow the light to shine past your physical body. Inhale and take in light, exhale and expand the light outward. Continue this cycle for a couple of minutes.

11. Just sit, breathing gently, in this radiant sphere of light. This light is not separate from you, it is the illumination of your personal energy that exists past the boundaries of your body.

12. Try to focus more on the feeling of the energy and less on the sensations of your skin. Can you eventually come to a state where the sensation of your body dissolves?

13. After a few minutes, bring your awareness back to your breath and body. How do your body, mind, emotions, or energy feel now? Has anything changed since the beginning of the meditation? Don't try to force anything. It may take several meditation sessions to notice real change, but take note of anything. Journaling is especially helpful during this process.

14. Then release the imagery and come back to your breath. Just breathe and feel the seat underneath you.

15. Take a few final deep breaths.

16. When you feel ready, open your eyes.
17. Take a few minutes to journal about your experience.

GREY | TRANSFORMATION

CHAPTER 17

GREY GEMSTONES TRANSFORMATION

GREY IS OFTEN CONSIDERED A NEUTRAL COLOR lacking in excitement. However, that could not be further from the truth. It is a color of potential. The color grey represents that which is hidden and can soon be revealed, like colors hidden in a darkened room. Wearing grey alongside another color causes that color to pop. Grey is a color that invites the revelation of something new and brilliant, just as you may have seen in the movie *The Wizard of Oz* when Dorothy's world changed from black-and-white to full color. You know something magical has just happened.

Grey is like the space inside a chrysalis before the butterfly emerges. It is like opening the door to a surprise party. It is the unknown moment before something new manifests. Grey feels like the eye of the storm, a still area of breathing room amid the chaos of change.

Grey is a color of mystery and magic. It is an invitation to peek behind the veil, to create from the ether, and to call up something from nothing, just like the apparently empty inside of a magician's hat. Grey is the space in which we can dream up something new for our lives. This could be a new job, new love, or a move to a city. The possibilities are endless from the energy of grey.

Grey gemstones help us turn our life in a different direction and progress in our life goals. Those drawn to grey gemstones are often seeking a transformation, support during a current change, or wanting to invite something new into their lives.

Grey Gemstones Help You Cultivate More . . .

Transformation

The flash and shimmer of stones like Labradorite and Larvikite, underscore the brightness waiting to emerge. It reminds us that situations can change; they can be different. We can emerge from a difficult situation with clarity, optimism, and inspiration.

Grey helps us recognize the need for change. When a situation is feeling dull, stagnant, or unhealthy, grey gems will inspire the search for something new. To bring a new sparkle and shine. It may be as simple as rearranging the furniture in a room to give it a different feel, or it could be as dramatic as changing your career direction. Meditation with a grey stone, such as Indigo Gabbro, will allow you to see the source of the dissatisfaction and to discover the optimum ways to invite change.

Grey gemstones help us find direction when we feel lost and adrift. If you're not sure what the next step in life should be, where you should be headed, or are seeking to discover your life purpose, then you are resting in the space of grey potential. Meditate with a grey gemstone to draw back the curtain obscuring the vision of your future. It helps to lift the fog and shine a light on your path. This enables you to transform the energy, direction, and purpose of your life.

Acceptance

Grey crystals are extremely supportive during times of change. Many people are deeply afraid of change, of the unknown, and of changing their routines and way of life. This is a completely normal and common experience.

There are various moments and experiences of change. For instance, when we know that it needs to occur but have yet to take that first step, like leaving an unhealthy relationship. Maybe transformation was unexpected and uninvited, like being laid off from a job, and we find ourselves swept up in its hectic energy. Shifts in life could be welcome but still overwhelm us with their enormity, such as having a baby. Changes don't always happen one at a time either. We could feel like we're in the ocean being battered by several forms of changes and need a life preserver. All of these flavors of change can cause anxiety, doubt, and fear. Grey gemstones can support you.

Grey is a color that is still, calm, and soothing. It provides a safe space, like a cocoon, to help us rest when we feel tired and overwhelmed by life's changes. Sit with a grey stone, such as Silver-Leaf Jasper to temporarily detach from the situation, bring yourself to the present moment, and just breathe.

Grey is also supportive when we are resistant to change. Suffering occurs when we are attached to something that no longer exists. We struggle against the current of life and can't accept the inevitable direction the river is taking. You could be holding onto the safe but unsatisfying job, to the former relationship or the lost opportunity, and this grasping can cause deep sorrow. This suffering can be released. Grey gemstones allow us to sit in its neutral energy to come to terms with the loss of something, or the unavoidable change.

Manifestation

When the energy of change and transformation is alive and active, it is the perfect time to manifest your hopes and dreams. We can design our own future, and if shifts are occurring, rather than struggle against them on the river of change, you can use your oars to guide and steer the direction. Aim your boat toward a satisfying outcome.

To manifest something is to set the intention for what you desire and to take action toward that outcome. It is to guide a dream from an idea in your heart and mind to a tangible item or activity. It is the act of intentionally inviting opportunity into your life. Manifestation applies to anything you would like to actively cultivate. Maybe you'd like to start a business, write a book, make that movie, increase your income, meet new people, plan a vacation, find a spiritual teacher, or anything you can possible dream up. Have a grey gemstone with you as you create vision boards, journal, meditate, and imagine the details of your vision. It helps to inspire creativity and strengthen your intentional energy toward making this goal happen. Hold the gemstone when you want the motivation to take active steps toward building your dream.

You can nurture and initiate manifestation even when change isn't imminent or actively occurring. If you feel the strong desire to make something happen in your life, then grey crystals will help you plan and initiate your aspirations. Maybe your life feels stagnant and dull. Grey gems can help you bring something new and exciting into your life, inspire purpose and direction, and enable you to be the director of your life experience. With grey gemstones you can enable your life to shine brilliantly.

Signs You Need More GREY Gemstone Energy

Try to incorporate grey gemstones into your daily Crystal Wisdom practice if you are experiencing the following symptoms or occurrences in your life.

- Seeking transformation and change
- Ready for something new to happen
- In the midst of a dramatic life change

- Wishing to stop struggling against the current change and invite peace
- Wanting to unveil your life purpose or destiny
- Deciding the next step in your life
- Would like to invite new opportunities into your life
- Wanting to manifest something into your life
- Trying to make a decision between new opportunities
- Feeling stuck and stagnant in life
- Feeling lost, adrift, and in need of direction

GREY GEMSTONES FOR TRANSFORMATION

These grey stones help initiate positive change and transformation, but also provide the unique supportive benefits listed below. Study these additional healing properties to help you identify the most appropriate stone to assist you.

Arfvedsonite – Stone of Rebirth: This gemstone supports transitions of all types, from large to small. This stone facilitates rebirth and change. Arfvedsonite provides the security and stability to initiate change, ride the waves of transformation, and to begin anew. It is a comforting stone during an end-of-life transition.

Covellite – Stone of Higher Self: This stone is used to awaken metaphysical abilities and open a channel for universal information. Covellite helps you to remain positive, enables you to turn dreams into concrete reality, and to see the miracles that surround you in life.

Fulgurite – Stone of Soul Healing: This stone, formed when lightning strikes sand, helps to heal and transform wounded parts of the soul. It aids recovery from past-life traumas that are blocking progress in this life. Helps you release ingrained beliefs and habits that are no longer serving you. Its lightning energy enables us to initiate great change and manifest our dreams.

Granite – Stone of Foresight: This is one of the most common rocks on the planet that is combined of various minerals. It touches to the heart of the Earth and provides deep stability and grounding. It enables you to see the big picture in all situations and be able to effectively determine the consequences of certain actions. It helps you determine the optimum path to your Highest Good.

Grey Moonstone – Stone of Reflection: It is balancing, introspective, reflective, and lunar. It allows you to absorb what is needed from the universe. It brings calm, focused awareness, and cleanses negativity from all the chakras. This stone helps you sink deeper into a contemplative, meditative state, and allows you to get in touch with your intuitive and feeling abilities rather than logic or reason. Moonstone is extremely nurturing; therefore, it helps to bring compassion and comfort to your life.

Indigo Gabbro (Mystic Merlinite) – Stone of Spiritual Journeying: This stone resonates to both the root and third eye chakra, so it will help ground you energetically while you open to the vast universe. Gabbro helps people enhance and develop all psychic and intuitive abilities. It allows you to safely journey into other dimensions, astral projections, dreams, and vision quests. It allows you to tap into the vast knowledge of the ethereal world.

Labradorite – Stone of Transformation and Magic: It is said to clear, balance, and protect the aura. It is purported to help provide clarity and insight into your destiny, as well as attract success. It is used in metaphysics for dream recall. Labradorite is said to increase

Chapter 17: GREY GEMSTONES | TRANSFORMATION 185

intuition, psychic development, esoteric wisdom, help with subconscious issues, and provide mental illumination.

Larvikite – Stone of Magic and Spellwork: This stone is beneficial in learning and developing all varieties of intuitive and magical abilities. It helps with meditation, journeying, visualizing, divination, spellwork, past life, and soul work. It grounds your physical self and protects you while you are in higher realms. Larvikite also dispels negativity and deflects spells aimed at the wearer. It assists with accepting divine timing and attunes us with the natural cycles of life.

Silver Sheen Obsidian – Stone of Introspection: Obsidian is a protective stone and forms a psychic barrier against attachments and psychic attacks. Silver-sheen is excellent for scrying, introspection, and will guide the soul back to the physical body during astral travel. It also helps us develop patience and perseverance to achieve our goals.

Spectrolite – Stone of Manifestation: The darker cousin of Labradorite, this stone will help to unveil your life purpose and destiny. It strengthens the clarity and intention of your aspirations and initiates powerful manifestation of your dreams. Spectrolite is said to increase intuition, psychic development, esoteric wisdom, help with subconscious issues, and provide mental illumination.

GEMSTONE MEDITATION FOR TRANSFORMATION

This is a guided meditation designed specifically to promote positive change with grey gemstones. If you are in need of new opportunities and direction, then identify a grey gemstone and try this crystal meditation. Go at your own pace, as you feel comfortable. The more familiar you are with the energy of your gemstone, the less time you may need to meditate to attain the benefits.

1. First, locate a grey gemstone to use during this meditation.
2. Find a comfortable place to sit. You can sit on a cushion on the floor, a chair, or directly on the ground outside. Make sure you can sit tall and comfortably for about ten to twenty minutes.
3. Hold the grey gemstone in your nondominant hand. This is your receiving hand that will take in the energy of the crystal.
4. Close your eyes and begin to take slow deep breaths.
5. Bring your awareness to where your legs and sitting bones are touching the floor or ground. Take a moment to feel the seat underneath you. You are completely supported and protected by the entire Earth underneath you.
6. Bring your attention to your body and take note of how your body, mind, emotions, and energy feel right now. Don't try to fix, change, or judge any experience, just take note. Be IN your body and see how it feels.
7. Now take a minute to feel the stone in your hand. Take note of its weight, smoothness, texture, and how it feels as you hold it.
8. Try to calm and settle your thinking mind. As you exhale, release any thoughts away on your breath.
9. Ask your Inner Guide, "Where do I desire change in my life?" Wait a minute or two for any guidance to arise.

10. Take note of any messages, words, images, or emotions that emerge.

11. Then ask your Inner Guide, "What is the change I need to make?" Wait a minute or two for any guidance to arise.

12. For more insight, ask your Inner Guide, "What options are available to me?" Wait a minute or two for any guidance to arise.

13. Then finally, for additional clarification, you can ask your Inner Guide, "Which option feels the best for my Highest Good?" Wait a minute or two for any guidance to arise.

14. After a few minutes, bring your awareness back to your breath and body. How do your body, mind, emotions, or energy feel now? Has anything changed since the beginning of the meditation? Don't try to force anything. It may take several meditation sessions to notice real change, but take note of anything. Journaling is especially helpful during this process.

15. Then release the imagery and come back to your breath. Just breathe and feel the seat underneath you.

16. Take a few final deep breaths.

17. When you feel ready, open your eyes.

18. Take a few minutes to journal about your experience.

PURPLE | INTUITION

CHAPTER 18

PURPLE GEMSTONES | INTUITION

Purple is associated with both the third eye and the crown chakras. These chakras guide our process of awakening and are the ignition for intuitive and spiritual awareness. This is a color that cultivates many layers of knowing and wisdom. The third eye chakra in particular strengthens our ability to tune into wisdom and use it in practical life situations.

Nina Ashby, in her book *Color Therapy: Plain & Simple*, says, "Violet is the combination of red and blue, which implies the spirit world taking charge over the physical plane." June Mcleod also describes purple as "transcendent of mind over matter, the higher self over the lower" in her book, *Colour Psychology Today*. Purple connects us to higher knowledge that can be gleaned outside of our physical five senses. The third eye enhances multiple ways of inner seeing, such as imagination and visualization, which allow us to connect with and perform meditations and spiritual practices. It bridges the thinking mind with inner wisdom.

Purple energy influences and strengthens the realm of inner, intuitive, and conscious knowing to broaden our scope of understanding. Those who are drawn to the color purple may be seeking support to develop their intuition, access their inner wisdom, and to apply their spiritual learning into their daily lives.

Purple Gemstones Help You Cultivate More . . .

Intuition

The color purple helps us to tap into and strengthen our sense of intuition. The term intuition refers to the sixth sense that provides us with a means of taking in additional information not associated with our physical five senses. It is used to describe those gut feelings and the innate knowing that doesn't rely on any proof for us to believe it. Intuition is our ability to interpret experiences from the world around us and develop a solid inner knowing to guide us. It enables us to know who to trust, or not. Intuition can let us know a situation isn't safe, that we should make a certain decision, or alter course.

The phrase "trusting your gut" is about the confidence we have in our intuition. A strong sense of intuition can guide us in healthy directions and keep us safe. If you don't feel you have a connection with your intuition, or that you don't trust what you feel, purple gemstones can help you sense and strengthen that relationship. Amethyst is a powerful stone for enhancing intuition. Sit with Amethyst with the specific intent to awaken your own intuition. Journal about your experiences in the meditation and about the glimpses of inner knowing you start to experience in your daily life.

The sense of intuition is the source for one's psychic abilities. To be psychic simply means to be able to receive and recognize signs and messages from outside the scope of our five senses. There is a wide range of skills that fall within this realm. Extrasensory perception, telepathy, empathy, divination, lucid dreaming, tarot reading, and mediumship are just a few examples. When you can open up and expand your intuitive knowing, you are able to enhance a focus area to receive guidance for yourself and others.

Inner Wisdom

Purple is the color of your inner wisdom. When you have developed a connection with your intuition, you can tap into your Inner Guide and inner wisdom with greater ease. As mentioned before, inner wisdom is that knowledge lying underneath the surface of our conscious thinking brain. Our surface thoughts and feelings can be so easily influenced by fear, bias, and social pressure. Inner wisdom is not affected by those influences. We access inner wisdom with a strong sense of intuition and by connecting to our Inner Guide. The Inner Guide is the part of yourself that knows exactly what you need to live a genuine, satisfying, and spirit enhancing life. Tapping into your Inner Guide and their offerings of inner wisdom will help you find the answers and solutions you have been seeking.

Your Inner Guide and inner wisdom are accessed most easily through meditation in a quiet space. Meditation is the doorway to inner wisdom. Working with purple crystals can strengthen your meditation practice. They make the practice easier to settle into. If you find it challenging to settle into meditation, then try your sessions holding a stone like Sugilite. Purple will help to calm your mind, ease distractions, release a sense of boredom, and enable you to just be.

This state of present being is that still, quiet space in which you can hear your Inner Guide. You will start to distinguish between "thinking brain" thoughts and inner wisdom. You will familiarize yourself with the sensation of active thinking that fuels the brain's desire to "figure it out" and then learn the gentle words, images, and impressions of your Inner Guide.

Practical Wisdom

Purple gemstones will then enable you to apply inner wisdom into everyday life. You can manifest the spiritual into the worldly.

Practical wisdom is about using our inner wisdom, intuitive discoveries, and higher guidance in our lives. It is about taking the spiritual and applying it to inspire transformation and change.

If you wish to change a deep-seated habit, sitting with Amethyst will help you discover the source of the behavior. Once you identify the root cause and trigger of the habit, you can figure out ways in which to release its grasp. Real transformation stems from changing behaviors at the course, not by exerting willpower on the symptoms. For example, I had a habit of snacking in the afternoon. It wasn't healthy for me and I wasn't even hungry, but I couldn't seem to break free from the routine. Just trying to avoid it didn't help at all. I sat with Amethyst and my inner wisdom helped me realize that I had a regular afternoon meeting that caused me some mild anxiety. I seemed to be snacking to relieve the anxiety. Once I made this discovery, I replaced the snacking with an afternoon meditation and was able to easily release the habit.

Wear or carry purple crystals with you to help you absorb spiritual knowledge and discover how to apply it in your daily life. This will help you use spiritual practices, meditations, and psychic information for practical transformation. For example, purple gems can help you absorb the energy of a meditation on compassion and then know exactly how to express deeper compassion toward others you encounter. If you received an intuitive warning, purple will aid you in deciphering the message and understanding how you can protect yourself.

The energy of purple influences the totality of wisdom in our lives. It enables us to access it, understand it, and use it in the most effective manner.

Signs You Need More PURPLE Gemstone Energy

Try to incorporate purple gemstones into your daily Crystal Wisdom practice if you are experiencing the following symptoms or occurrences in your life.

- Starting a meditation practice
- Finding it challenging to sit for meditation
- Wanting to deepen and strengthen your spiritual practices
- Wishing to tap into extrasensory and psychic abilities
- Having difficulty tapping into your intuition
- Not trusting your intuition
- Seeking answers to life questions within
- Having an ethical dilemma
- Wanting to live a life based on your spiritual values

PURPLE GEMSTONES FOR AWAKENING INTUITION

These purple stones open up your soul to receive light and guidance from the universe, but also provide the unique supportive benefits listed below. Study these additional healing properties to help you identify the most appropriate stone to assist you.

Amethyst – Stone of Spirituality and Contentment: It balances the energies of the intellectual, emotional, and physical bodies and provides a clear connection between the earthly plane and other worlds. It clears the aura and stabilizes and transmutes any dysfunctional energies. Amethyst represents the principles of complete metamorphosis. It aids against addictions, and increases stability, strength, energy, and peace.

Ametrine – Stone of Spiritual Abundance: This is a combination of Amethyst and Citrine, so it combines many of their qualities. Ametrine helps you connect deeply to Spirit with assurance and optimism. The cleansing attributes of Citrine are amplified and sped up by the power of Amethyst. This helps to releases any negative blockages and behavior programming that stand in the way of your best life. It increases compatibility, cooperation, and harmony in your relationships.

Charoite – Stone of Transformation and Acceptance: Charoite helps you through times of immense change. This stone helps you to release great fear and to look at your current situation in a calm manner. It helps you to accept the present and make wise decisions that are not based in fear reactions. Charoite helps to transmute negative energies, and to understand better those who are immersed in negativity, allowing for deeper compassion and acceptance. Any negativity you pick up from others will be transformed and will not bring you down with it. Because of its transmutation qualities, it is a natural auric cleansing stone.

Fluorite – Stone of Order and Learning: Fluorite brings order to chaos. Its energy stabilizes and connects the mind, body, heart, and spirit energies. Being multi-colored, it helps to balance and clear all the chakras and energetic channels, allowing one to open to guidance from spirit. Fluorite is also an amazing study aid! It helps to sharpen the mind, increase focus and memory, and aids in the absorption of information.

Iolite – Stone of Intuition: Iolite is used often during spiritual practices, (such as healing, guided meditation, journeying, and astral projection) as it strengthens the third eye. It heightens intuitive abilities and accuracy of visions. It can help you move painlessly through change. Iolite aligns and balances all the fields of the aura.

Lepidolite – Stone of Transition: Its energy helps you through times of change. It also helps awaken and open the crown chakra, allowing you to become aware of the inner and outer energies. This is an incredibly soothing stone and is very useful to reduce stress and anxiety. It dispels negativity and lifts depression.

Purple Aventurine – Stone of the Spirit: All Aventurine is very healing, restores energies within you, and protects from energetic attachments. Purple Aventurine, in particular, supports you during spiritual decisions and when recovering from spiritual disappointments.

Phosphosiderite – Stone of Soul Work: This stone helps you to access Akashic records and past life information. This aids in understanding your soul path and your purpose, not just in this life, but in your multi-life existence. It helps you to resolve karmic debt to smooth the way for growth and deeper wisdom in the future. As this also works with the heart, it brings forth the understanding that all beings are interconnected and encourages compassion and cooperation on a spiritual level. As you raise your vibration, you help to raise the vibration of all.

Purpurite – Stone of Enlightenment: This gemstone connects the crown chakra to the root, allows complete energetic opening of your intuition, and stimulates efforts toward enlightenment. Purpurite also provides powerful psychic protection and guards against ill wishes from others. It also removes barriers on your spiritual journey. This could be past-life blocks, interference from others, self-doubt, and emotional resistance.

Stichtite – **Stone of True Self:** Stichtite is a stone that encourages you to live fully and openly as your most authentic and highest self. It encourages incorporating compassion and love into all decisions. It also highlights the effects of negative thoughts, speech, or a negative attitude in your own mindset. It shows you that positive, optimistic thoughts and actions will guide you naturally to your Highest Good.

Sugilite – **Stone of Incarnation:** This is a stone that reminds you why we incarnated on the Earth in this human experience. It helps you find answers to questions like, "Why am I here?" and "Where did I come from?" It supports all those who do not feel like they quite "fit" where they are. This is a love stone that helps you love yourself as you are, love your existence, have peaceful connections with others, and to heal from major wounds and traumas.

Tanzanite – **Stone of Magic:** Tanzanite enhances the balance between personal power, creativity, will, and actualization, so you can bring your dreams to reality. It stimulates visions and insight into your higher goals. It has also been used to enable communication with the spirit world.

GEMSTONE MEDITATION FOR AWAKENING INTUITION

This is a guided meditation designed specifically to awaken intuitive energy using purple gemstones. If you are in need of inner wisdom and guidance, then identify a purple gemstone and try this crystal meditation. Go at your own pace, as you feel comfortable. The more familiar you are with the energy of your gemstone, the less time you may need to meditate to attain the benefits.

1. First, locate a purple gemstone to use during this meditation.
2. Find a comfortable place to sit. You can sit on a cushion on the floor, a chair, or directly on the ground outside. Make sure you can sit tall and comfortably for about ten to twenty minutes.
3. Hold the purple gemstone in your nondominant hand. This is your receiving hand that will take in the energy of the crystal.
4. Close your eyes and begin to take slow deep breaths.
5. Bring your awareness to where your legs and sitting bones are touching the floor or ground. Take a moment to feel the seat underneath you. You are completely supported and protected by the entire Earth underneath you.
6. Bring your attention to your body and take note of how your body, mind, emotions, and energy feel right now. Don't try to fix, change, or judge any experience, just take note. Be IN your body and see how it feels.
7. Now take a minute to feel the stone in your hand. Take note of its weight, smoothness, texture, and how it feels as you hold it.
8. Try to relax your shoulders and your mind. Relaxing your shoulders helps to draw tension from your forehead.
9. As you exhale, release any thoughts away with your breath. Continue this until your mind feels calm and still.
10. Bring a question or situation to mind for which you would like an answer.

11. Release the desire to let your brain "figure it out." Allow your Inner Guide to offer you guidance. Notice how the information arises for you. It could be with words, images, impressions, emotions, or sounds. Part of this practice is for you to learn the language of your Inner Guide.

12. If you notice that your mind is working, trying to answer or resolve it for you, then exhale and breathe those thoughts away.

13. If you need to repeat the question, then do so and wait quietly. Allow the guidance to arise from within.

14. If you would like some clarification or additional information, ask your guide, "Please tell me more."

15. After you feel you've received your wisdom, bring your awareness back to your breath and body. How do your body, mind, emotions, or energy feel now? Has anything changed since the beginning of the meditation? Don't try to force anything. It may take several meditation sessions to notice real change but take note of anything. Journaling is especially helpful during this process.

16. Then release the imagery and come back to your breath. Just breathe and feel the seat underneath you.

17. Take a few final deep breaths.

18. When you feel ready, open your eyes.

19. Take a few minutes to journal about your experience.

20. Take note of any signs, signals, or messages in your daily life after you perform this meditation. The guidance may still arise well after the meditation is finished.

WHITE | CLEANSING

CHAPTER 19

WHITE GEMSTONES | CLEANSING

WHITE REFLECTS THE ENTIRE COLOR SPECTRUM and provides us with a complete balanced exposure to all colors and shades. In this regard it is incredibly cleansing and soothing to our entire living system. It cleanses the energetic body and aura, soothes our emotions, purifies our spiritual being, and much like the shining rays of the sun, provides nourishment to our body.

White is a color that, in the West, commonly represents cleanliness and purity. White is "as pure as the driven snow." It is the color of white linens, white gloves, and laboratory coats. This is to highlight the utter cleanliness in those environments.

White will put flaws and dirt on display. This may seem like a negative feature, but it allows us to contemplate and resolve that which might be holding us back on our spiritual path. It highlights areas for reflection and self-discovery. It enables us to cleanse and purify our soul.

Those attracted to white gemstones are often seeking energetic cleansing, spiritual clarity, and the soothing space of inner peace.

White Gemstones Will Help You Cultivate More . . .

Cleansing

The full color spectrum of white is extremely cleansing to our energy and environment. It is useful for cleansing your aura energy, the energy of a room, a mood, and even other gemstones. The radiance of white shines through all accumulated energy to leave it feeling crisp and clear.

Use a combination of white gemstones and white candles to freshen the energy of a room. These can be combined with the incenses of Sage and Palo Santo to provide a spiritual cleansing for people, places, and gemstones. This practice is especially useful if you are moving into a new home, office space, and meditation area. It will remove the accumulated energies of the previous occupants and leave a blank, clean slate for your presence.

White gemstones are extremely useful to clear and cleanse the energies of other gemstones. Crystals that are frequently used will absorb and accumulate the energies you are releasing. I recommend clearing your gemstones on a regular basis to release those old energies from the stones. Place a white stone, such as White Calcite or Selenite, near your crystals to cleanse and freshen their energy.

Meditate with white crystals to cleanse and rejuvenate your own energy field. Imagine the white light of the gemstone filling your energetic body and dissolving any accumulated and stagnant energies. The practice should leave you feeling alert, refreshed, and radiant.

Purity

White helps us live in a state of purity. This does not mean that we are flawless and free of stain, but that we are trying to live in accordance with our spiritual ideals and values. This means you have confidence in your spiritual values and can make decisions based on your knowledge, experience, and faith. Choices and actions are taken not as a reaction from fear but considered carefully from a place of courage and compassion. Purity is the act of taking the time to consider if an action is in line with your spiritual beliefs. Purity does not imply that one is perfect, but that we actively consider the spiritual consequences of our actions and make decisions based on what we believe to be spiritually supportive. Then we have compassion with ourselves when we have difficulty with that.

Meditating with white stones helps to develop our spiritual values and live our lives by those values. Spiritual values encourage us to aspire to live life to support our Highest Good. Your Highest Good is the state of being in which your life actions and goals are in line with your authentic spiritual values. When you choose to live a life that lifts the quality, compassion, equanimity, and optimism in the world that is living for your Highest Good. White gems help you reflect on life and spiritual experiences to identify the life lessons. It enables you to use wisdom to handle situations differently in the future. In addition, white helps you resolve ethical dilemmas by tuning into your inner wisdom for guidance.

Peace

When we touch into soul qualities like love, compassion, empathy, kindness, and the higher purpose that shapes our spiritual values, we naturally cultivate more inner peace and harmony within. This is a color that helps us make peace with decisions and life situations because we are confident we can maneuver these according to our heart and spirit. This cultivates a sense of deep, unshakeable inner peace.

White inspires a sense of quiet that is simple, clear, and balanced. When we sit with white gemstones, we can release harsh emotions, frustrations, and impatience. These emotions no longer have a hold on our mind and heart, so they melt and dissolve from our being. Sit with a white stone, like Howlite, when you feel overwhelmed by difficult emotions. Imagine them melting down into the nurturing Earth or away from you on your breath. Feel the ease settle into your heart, body, and energy. Sit in the quiet, balanced energy of white.

White is the color of the dove, which represents peace between people. White gemstones can cultivate harmony and understanding between people. It helps to release tension between people and to dissolve energetic barriers between them. This opens a pathway for genuine, heartfelt communication. White is the color of surrender and can encourage us to set down opinions and feelings which we are clinging to that are fracturing and damaging the relationship. Wear or carry white gems with you when you need to have a conversation with someone you have had a tense relationship with.

White gemstones help balance our energy, values, and emotions to promote an environment of expansive peace and harmony. These stones help to settle and calm us on all levels of our being.

Signs You Need More WHITE Gemstone Energy

Try to incorporate white gemstones into your daily Crystal Wisdom practice if you are experiencing the following symptoms or occurrences in your life.

- Desiring a total energetic cleansing
- Feeling tired and sluggish
- Needing to clear a room of heavy or negative feelings
- Moving into a new home, office space, or spiritual practice area
- Cleansing your gemstone collection
- Wanting to live by your fundamental spiritual ideals
- Having difficulty making a spiritual decision
- Experiencing a moral or ethical dilemma

- Wanting to cultivate inner peace and harmony
- Needing to relax
- Wanting to inspire peace in a relationship

WHITE GEMSTONES FOR CLEANSING

These white stones help to cleanse all varieties of energy in your life, but also provide the unique supportive benefits listed below. Study these additional healing properties to help you identify the most appropriate stone to assist you.

Howlite – Stone of Calming: Howlite is an extremely soothing and calming stone. It helps to dissipate any anger you hold, or anger directed toward you. It helps to stimulate ambition and is a perfect stone to wear when you are trying to take action on an idea or project. Helps you keep working on a long-term project or goal when you have lost motivation and perseverance.

Opal – Stone of Karma: This is a very gentle stone. It is cleansing, soothing, and nurturing. It helps to gently stimulate psychic vision and abilities. It is a stone of karma. It amplifies what we receive and manifest and sends it back out to the world. It teaches that what you put out into the world is what comes back to you. In that vein, Opal encourages generosity and optimism as a way to nurture ourselves and others.

Rainbow Moonstone – Stone of Reflection: It is balancing, introspective, reflective, and lunar. It allows you to absorb what is needed from the universe. It brings calm, focused awareness, and cleanses negativity from all the chakras. This stone helps you sink deeper into a contemplative, meditative state, and allows you to get in touch with your intuitive and feeling abilities rather than logic or reason. Rainbow Moonstone is feminine and nurturing; therefore, helping to bring compassion and comfort to your life.

Scolecite – Stone of Universal Connection: Scolecite can gently enhance meditative and dream states. It helps you connect with universal, intuitive, angelic, and ancient sources of wisdom. The peace energies of Scolecite are far-reaching and can help one learn gentleness, inner peace, living from the heart with peace, and lack of fear. It helps to connect the energies of people and groups, transforming conflict into peace. It can help you take control of life so that what you want can be manifested.

Selenite – Stone of Cleansing: Selenite exudes a powerful cleansing, protective, and opening energy. It will purify a room's energy and will also cleanse gems and crystals it is stored with. It is valuable to use in a meditation room when you are trying to connect to deeper wisdom or past lives. Selenite stores knowledge of the past and future, so focused meditation can unlock that insight.

Ulexite – Stone of Inner Focus: This crystal is one that magnifies intentions and energies in your life. It brings issues into clear focus, allowing for understanding and resolution. It enables you to understand the messages from your spirit guides, dreams, and intuition. It shows you your true path and what is blocking you along the way.

White Agate – Stone of Enlightenment: White Agate helps you connect deeply with the energies of the universe and the Earth to guide and support you on the path to awakening and enlightenment. This stone encourages mindfulness and introspection. It also helps you to cut cords with negative past relationships. When used in the home, it can repel unwanted spirits.

White Aventurine – Stone of Cleansing: All Aventurine is very healing, restores energies within us, and protects from energetic attachments. White Aventurine is especially cleansing. It purifies your energy, aura, intentions, and environment. It also cleanses your heart of the lingering residue from old wounds.

White Calcite – Stone of Spiritual Awakening: This gemstone is a powerful cleanser and amplifier of energy. Just having Calcite in a room will clear it of all negative energies. It invigorates stagnant energy in the body. This crystal facilitates the awakening of all intuitive and psychic abilities and accelerates spiritual development. This stone also helps to strengthen emotional intelligence.

White (Snow) Quartz – Stone of Life Lessons: Snow Quartz helps you to look at what you're experiencing and truly learn the lesson from it. It helps to create and maintain personal boundaries and overcome feelings of victimhood. This gemstone helps you consider your message before speaking to be able to deliver the most effective message. Snow Quartz also enables deeper meditation and access to inner wisdom.

GEMSTONE MEDITATION FOR CLEANSING

This is a guided meditation designed specifically to promote energy cleansing using white gemstones. If you are in need of soothing, balancing, and cleansing, then identify a white gemstone and try this crystal meditation. Go at your own pace, as you feel comfortable. The more familiar you are with the energy of your gemstone, the less time you will need to meditate to attain the benefits.

1. First, locate a white gemstone to use during this meditation.
2. Find a comfortable place to sit. You can sit on a cushion on the floor, a chair, or directly on the ground outside. Make sure you can sit tall and comfortably for about ten to twenty minutes.
3. Hold the white gemstone in your nondominant hand. This is your receiving hand that will take in the energy of the crystal.
4. Close your eyes and begin to take slow deep breaths.
5. Bring your awareness to where your legs and sitting bones are touching the floor or ground. Take a moment to feel the seat underneath you. You are completely supported and protected by the entire Earth underneath you.
6. Bring your attention to your body and take note of how your body, mind, emotions, and energy feel right now. Don't try to fix, change, or judge any experience, just take note. Be IN your body and see how it feels.
7. Now take a minute to feel the stone in your hand. Take note of its weight, smoothness, texture, and how it feels as you hold it.
8. Imagine a bright light shining on the very top crown of your head.
9. As you inhale, imagine drawing this light energy down into the middle of your body. Take ten deep breaths like this, drawing down the energy.

10. As you breathe, imagine your body filling with this radiant, white energy.
11. The white energy will dissolve any dark, stagnant, or heavy energy within you.
12. If you are holding onto harsh or difficult emotions, allow them to dissolve in the light.
13. If you are feeling physical tensions, let the light melt them away as well, leaving you feeling relaxed, calm, and at peace.
14. Allow yourself to sit in this space of peace for a few minutes.
15. After a few minutes, bring your awareness back to your breath and body. How does your body, mind, emotions, or energy feel now? Has anything changed since the beginning of the meditation? Don't try to force anything. It may take several meditation sessions to notice real change, but take note of anything. Journaling is especially helpful during this process.
16. Then release the imagery and come back to your breath. Just breathe and feel the seat underneath you.
17. Take a few final deep breaths.
18. When you feel ready, open your eyes.
19. Take a few minutes to journal about your experience.

CLEAR | ENERGY

CHAPTER 20

CLEAR GEMSTONES | ENERGY BODY

THIS FINAL COLOR MAY SEEM TRICKY, and you could be wondering, "How could I possibly be attracted to *clear*?" But one can certainly find oneself drawn to clear gemstones, and it can have a powerful impact on your crystal practice and your life experience.

Clear is a color of transparency and openness. There is nothing to hide here because we can see through it all. We can see through glass windows, doors, and walls so we don't feel closed off from the world around us. It reminds us that the boundaries of the physical human body don't limit our expansive energetic being.

You may find yourself attracted to clear glass dishes, crystal dishes, rooms with lots of windows, and glass furniture. This is a color that represents pure, unadulterated energy. Those attracted to clear gemstones may be seeking a stronger, healthier connection with their personal energy and to share in the energetic experience with others on this human journey.

Clear Gemstones Will Help You Cultivate More...

Energy Amplification

Clear gemstones represent the clear luminosity of our energetic body. Many clear gems have a sparkle and shimmer of rainbow colors as the light shines through like a prism. This is how our energy body appears as well. Our energy is clear with some colors that reflect the unique attributes of our aura.

These gemstones help us tap into our energy system. Clear crystals are especially effective for Reiki, Quantum, and other types of energy healers. These stones help you connect to the healing energy and amplify the strength of the energy you channel to yourself and your clients. Wear or hold a clear crystal to focus, direct, and intensify the energy flow. I often use Clear Quartz for in-person and distance Reiki healing sessions, as well as when I am teaching Reiki and giving empowerments to students.

Clear crystals are also very useful for energy movement practices such as feng shui, chakra balancing, yoga, Qi Gong, Tai Chi, or acupuncture. Wear a crystal, such as Danburite, when you are going to teach, perform, or receive an energy session. A bracelet is helpful if you are doing movement practices because it won't drape in front of your face in yoga, or fall out of your pocket during other Tai Chi or Qi Gong exercises.

If you are interested in learning energy work, or want to strengthen a current practice, clear gemstones will enable you to tap into the sensation of your personal energy with ease. They are beneficial for both students and teachers.

Energetic Health

Working with clear gemstones also heals and strengthens your aura. If you feel a lack of energy, or feel off-balance, and you're not sure why, there could be a weak area or leak in your aura. The leak allows your energy to drain out rather than being contained within your energetic body.

You can also feel tired or adrift if your energy is not flowing smoothly throughout your body. If there is an energy block, it can cause a disruption in energy movement, causing energy to build up in one area and deplete another. Sometimes lack of energy work causes stagnancy within your system. Just as we may feel sluggish if we haven't exercised lately, we can also feel tired if we haven't performed energy practices recently. Meditate with a gemstone like Herkimer Diamond to visualize your energy flowing smoothly and balanced throughout your system. The energy practices just discussed, such as yoga, are also effective methods of giving your energy body a workout.

Clear gemstones help you familiarize yourself with your energy fields. If you are just starting to work with your aura or energy body, crystals can help you sense the bounds, colors, and wellness of your own aura. Regular work sensing and moving your personal energy can keep your energy body healthy.

Being as One

Clear crystals will also help you discover and embrace your own divine nature. The brilliant, shining Diamond within. In the Buddhist Diamond Sutra, the Diamond is used as a metaphor to illustrate the means by which we can be free from illusions. Specifically, the illusion that we are individuals, separate from each other. It cultivates a perception of nonduality, which is a view that we are not separated or divided from others. We are all one.

The clear color represents a lack of boundaries between us and others. All sentient beings experience joy, pain, regret, and love, among all other emotions. We all wish to avoid suffering and to cultivate happiness in our lives. When we realize that we all share this common human experience, it enables compassion, empathy, and connection to develop with any other person we encounter. It eases frustration and increases patience, but we understand deeply that the other person also experiences human suffering.

If you are feeling like a small cog in a huge world, clear gemstones help you connect to the vastness of the universe. Stones such as

Danburite unite you with the energy of infinite space and enable you to feel part of a collective experience. Our personal energies have no bounds. Your energy melds with another's energy and this continues across the globe and throughout space. All energy is one. Once again, I say that we are all human beings together with shared energy, emotions, suffering, and joys. Clear gemstones cultivate human connection and peace.

Signs You Need More CLEAR Gemstone Energy

Try to incorporate clear gemstones into your daily Crystal Wisdom practice if you are experiencing the following symptoms or occurrences in your life.

- Are an energy worker or Reiki healer
- Wanting to strengthen your abilities to work with your personal energy
- Performing a practice that moves and manipulates energy
- Feeling a lack of energy or balance and aren't sure why
- Needing to strengthen or heal your aura
- Wanting to connect with your divine nature
- Would like to feel more connection to the energy of humanity
- Wanting to experience the feeling of being one with all
- Studying or practicing nonduality

CLEAR GEMSTONES FOR AMPLIFYING ENERGY

These clear stones help to amplify all varieties of energy in your life but also provide the unique supportive benefits listed below. Study these additional healing properties to help you identify the most appropriate stone to assist you.

Apophyllite – Stone of Acceptance: This crystal is an incredible conductor of electricity. It amplifies all energies within a person, room, or group of people. It helps you connect with your radiant divine nature and releases concern about flaws or weaknesses. Apophyllite helps you feel comfortable in your body, accessing the spirit world, and supports out-of-body practices.

Clear Calcite – Stone of New Beginnings: This gemstone is a powerful cleanser and amplifier of energy. Just having Calcite in a room will clear it of all negative energies. It invigorates stagnant energy in the body. This crystal facilitates the awakening of all intuitive and psychic abilities and accelerates spiritual development. Clear Calcite is a stone of new beginnings and fresh starts.

Clear Quartz – Stone of Amplification: Clear Quartz is known as the "master healer" and will amplify energy and thought, as well as the effect of other crystals. It absorbs, stores, releases, and regulates energy. Clear Quartz draws off negative energy of all kinds. Clear Quartz enhances psychic abilities, harmonizes all the chakras, and aligns the subtle bodies.

Clear Topaz – Stone of Karma: This gemstone enables you to be aware of the karmic effects of your actions. It allows you to see the big picture and your impact on this world. It removes stagnant energy, which helps you feel rejuvenated.

Danburite – **Stone of Authenticity:** This stone encourages you to let your light shine and appreciate your authentic self! It is one of the highest vibration stones and helps to ease worry and stress. It helps to release emotional pain and boost self-esteem. Danburite can help heal old deep wounds, as well as clear past karma. It helps to bring the aspects of enlightenment and love toward realization.

Diamond – **Stone of Manifestation:** The Diamond is a powerful stone. It enhances relationships and marks commitment in marriages. It attracts abundance and enables you to manifest positivity and optimal opportunities into your life. It purifies the aura and allows your light to shine through to the world! Diamonds help to ease fear and shine a light in the darkness. It also amplifies energy and the effects of other stones.

Girasol Quartz – **Stone of Phobias:** This gemstone connects you deeply with your karmic and past-life issues, especially regarding how these affect your present life. Girasol is most effective at helping you identify the root cause of phobias. Many intense fears can seem unfounded, but actually have roots in a past life issue. The karmic blocks need to be addressed and resolved for the phobia to fade.

Herkimer Diamond – **Stone of Attunement:** This crystal can be used to attune the wearer to another person, environment, or spiritual practice. It helps you to "be" in the present moment, allowing the necessary surrender and/or strength to just sit with the situation and learn its lesson or wisdom. Herkimer Diamonds help you attain a new beginning in this lifetime. It brings fresh starts when needed.

Icelandic Spar (Optical Calcite) – **Stone of Clarity:** This gemstone is a powerful cleanser and amplifier of energy. Just having Calcite in a room will clear it of all negative energies. It invigorates stagnant energy in the body. This crystal helps us to see through our own personal and emotional projections and to see the clear truth.

Lodolite Quartz – Stone of Serenity: This gemstone appears like a beautiful garden inside Quartz and helps you maintain physical and inner safe spaces. It allows you to feel peace, harmony, and serenity as you visualize a relaxing, secure place. It also helps to manifest this peace into your everyday life.

GEMSTONE MEDITATION FOR ENERGY AMPLIFICATION

This is a guided meditation designed specifically to amplify energy work using clear gemstones. If you are in need of energy balancing and healing, then identify a clear gemstone and try this crystal meditation. Go at your own pace, as you feel comfortable. The more familiar you are with the energy of your gemstone, the less time you may need to meditate to attain the benefits.

1. First, locate a clear gemstone to use during this meditation.
2. Find a comfortable place to sit. You can sit on a cushion on the floor, a chair, or directly on the ground outside. Make sure you can sit tall and comfortably for about ten to twenty minutes.
3. Hold the clear gemstone in your nondominant hand. This is your receiving hand that will take in the energy of the crystal.
4. Close your eyes and begin to take slow deep breaths.

5. Bring your awareness to where your legs and sitting bones are touching the floor or ground. Take a moment to feel the seat underneath you. You are completely supported and protected by the entire Earth underneath you.
6. Bring your attention to your body and take note of how your body, mind, emotions, and energy feel right now. Don't try to fix, change, or judge any experience, just take note. Be IN your body and see how it feels.
7. Now take a minute to feel the stone in your hand. Take note of its weight, smoothness, texture, and how it feels as you hold it.
8. Imagine a bright light shining on the very top crown of your head.
9. As you inhale, imagine drawing this light energy down into the middle of your body. Take ten deep breaths like this, drawing down the energy.
10. Then as you exhale, imagine the energy expanding as beyond the physical bounds of your body. Continue this cycle for another ten breaths.
11. Notice where the energy seems to fade out when you are expanding it out. This is the current boundary of your energetic body. All the energy outside of your skin is your aura.
12. As you breathe in and out, drawing in energy and breathing it out, notice how your aura looks and feels to you. Notice any areas that seem thin, weak, or cracked. How this looks or feels is unique to everyone; get to know how your aura looks to you.

13. As you exhale, allow a little more energy to flow to any parts in your aura that need reinforcement. Do this until your aura feels balanced, solid, and whole.

14. After a few minutes, bring your awareness back to your breath and body. How do your body, mind, emotions or energy feel now? Has anything changed since the beginning of the meditation? Don't try to force anything. It may take several meditation sessions to notice real change, but take note of anything. Journaling is especially helpful during this process.

15. Then release the imagery and come back to your breath. Just breathe and feel the seat underneath you.

16. Take a few final deep breaths.

17. When you feel ready, open your eyes.

18. Take a few minutes to journal about your experience.

CHAPTER 21

EVOLVING YOUR CRYSTAL COLOR PRACTICE

THE PREVIOUS CHAPTERS ABOUT THE BENEFITS of crystal colors are designed to be a regular reference and guide during your daily life. Whenever you feel the call of a particular color, consult that chapter to help you uncover the insight it may be offering. Sit with a gemstone of that color to tap into your own inner wisdom. Allow the color of gemstones to provide you with understanding, guidance, resolution, and inspiration to take control of your life and respond in an informed and intentional manner.

To gain optimum benefit from adding color wisdom to your Crystal Wisdom practice, I encourage you to take a few steps that will enable you to uplift and transform your life experience. Practicing, journaling, and embracing color in your life will initiate powerful life improvements.

Practice Regularly

The information offered in this book is meant to help you listen to your Inner Guide and *take action*. It is meant to be used and incorporated into your life so you can make powerful improvements. Crystal colors can help you make more meaningful decisions, actions, and intentions. They support life changes that will improve the ease and satisfaction with which you live your life. But this only works if you practice regularly. If you actively work with your gemstones, tap into your inner wisdom, and take actions based on that information.

To begin, make the intention to notice the colors in your day from the moment you wake up. Take mindful care as you reach for clothing to wear that day. Ask yourself, "Why was I drawn to wear grey today?" Make notes of color choices in your journal. You may even carry a small, pocket-sized notebook with you in your pocket or purse to take notes about colors as you navigate your day. I don't intend for this practice to be burdensome or overwhelming, so just notice what stands out to you during the day. What piques the interest of your intuition? You don't have to take immediate action for every color you encounter but writing it down will help you notice trends over time.

Also, notice which gemstones you are reaching for. Which ones draw your eye as you pass your crystal display? Which crystals popped up on your favorite crystal websites or social media platforms? Do the benefits of that gemstone color resonate with you? Does it bring to mind a situation you are dealing with? Write in your journal what you feel your daily color messages might be.

If you feel a connection with a particular color and you feel it has a message relevant to your life, write that down. Notice where you see the examples of that reflected in your life. Take some time to sit and consider that life situation. For example, I recently noticed that I was wearing more grey clothing than normal. For more than a week, I was choosing grey over any other color in my wardrobe and wearing silver and grey shoes to match. When that realization struck me, I asked myself if I happened to be in a time of transformation. The answer was an immediate, "Yes!"

I had just launched my first book and was making an internal and professional transition to being a published author. My Inner

Guide recognized that I was undergoing this change and I had been reaching for grey clothing to support my energy during this life change. I knew then that I needed to take time to honor this transformation and recognize it for the important milestone that it was. I sat and meditated with Labradorite to absorb and accept the energy of transition and transformation. I felt the deep authenticity of this moment resonate within my body and energy. I knew I was on the right path. Recognizing the message of the color grey helped me to honor and appreciate this very special time period.

If you have utilized Crystal Color Wisdom in your life, record this in your journal as well. I wrote down my experience with grey and transformation so I could document that I acknowledged and acted upon my inner wisdom. These actions lead to transformation and change, so taking notes of these moments are valuable to reinforce the powerful effects of your practice.

If you'd like even more information about a particular color occurrence, then choose a gemstone of that color and perform the crystal color meditation from Chapter 7. What does your Inner Guide have to say about the meaning of that color? If it doesn't appear to be relevant to your life at the time, write it down in your journal for future reference. Notice, meditate, reflect, and write. This is the recipe for alchemy in your life.

Review Your Journal Notes

The next recommendation is to reserve some time on a regular basis to review the notes in your journal. Reviewing your journal is a valuable time of reflection on your daily experiences.

Every one or two weeks, sit down in a quiet place and look through the contents of your journal (or your color notebook if your carry one with you). Notice if any color repeats more than the others. Notice if any themes repeat or stand out to you. During the hectic activities of your day, it may be difficult to notice what the colors and signs from our Inner Guide might mean, but as we look at the information over time, trends and themes may rise to the surface. We are able to make connections between occurrences day by day and see the current of a life theme emerging. This is only possible with intentional reflection.

Maybe this theme is large enough in your life that you decide to add this color gemstone to your Guardian Gemstone team. Consider consulting my previous book, *Crystal Wisdom*, and building a daily practice with this gemstone. Then you can start incorporating daily and spontaneous practices based on the signs and messages from color wisdom you have noticed. This will introduce potent, intentional transformation. Reviewing your journal helps you recognize when new, significant life needs arise and how you can incorporate a new gemstone into your regular meditation practices.

Reading back in your journal will also highlight the powerful changes taking place. You will be able to see the journey as you noticed that pink, for example, made a positive impact in your life. Perhaps you noticed that you bought a few more pink items than normal. You took note of that in your journal. Then you reflected that the theme of pink is love and considered where love may be making an appearance in your life. You meditated with Rose Quartz to realize that there has been someone new in your life expressing interest, but you hadn't initially noticed it. Then you made the choice to speak to that person more and get to know them. This positive change could pass unnoticed as it unfolded in your life, but when you read back through your notes in your journal, the undeniable record of this positive life change took form in your written word. This reinforces the value of hearing your inner wisdom and taking action based on its truth.

Revisit the Color Chapters

This book is meant to be a reference for your everyday life. Whenever you notice a color's increasing appearance in your life, you can review its chapter in Part 2 to help you reflect on the color message to you. Read through the list of symptoms to see if any seem familiar to you. Review the three benefits, sit with your gemstone, and tap into your inner wisdom for life revelations. How can this color help you make positive life changes?

In reverse, you can also incorporate a color into your life to support a current life need. Do you feel you need more energy and stimulation? The chapter on red can help you identify exactly where you may need some extra energy and which gemstone can support you in generating extra vitality. The gemstone meditation in each chapter will help to initiate that process within you and to take that color energy out into your daily life.

Embrace the Beauty and Wisdom of Colors

And finally, have fun with colors and your gemstones! Breathe in the luscious energy of crystal colors, allow them to seep into your energy and to brighten your days. Enjoy shopping for new crystals and pay attention to the particular shades that draw your eye. Pick up different color stones and see how they make you feel. Display them where you can absorb their energy through your eyes when you look at them. Then, of course, pick them up and use them when needed. Allow the radiance of colors to uplift and brighten your life!

CHAPTER 22

WRAPPING UP

I HOPE YOU HAVE ENJOYED your exploration through the world of Crystal Color Wisdom. I offer this resource as a tool to help you notice and appreciate the signs from your Inner Guide and higher sources. Hopefully, you will see the color in your daily life with a new appreciation and regularly tap into the guidance it has to offer. Consider it a palette of signs and messages from your inner knowing to enable you to live your best life. Learning the powerful meanings of the colors that catch your attention will help you strengthen your relationship to your own Inner Guide. It will strengthen your connection to your crystal collection and Guardian Gemstones to experience more effective and fruitful meditation sessions.

Incorporating Crystal Color Wisdom into your everyday life will help you live with more mindfulness and attention to everything around you. When consistently noticing and journaling about the color influences each day, you take an active role in choosing the direction and intention of your days. This action steers your life in a more meaningful and rewarding direction. You will be intentionally listening to your inner wisdom, making choices that are healthy and authentic, and living life in accordance with your true purpose and passions.

The act of paying attention to colors also helps you to experience the beauty in everything surrounding you. You will notice the brilliant color of flowers, artwork, architecture, animals, and clothing. You can choose to envelope yourself in nurturing colors when you dress and choose décor for your home. You may view your crystal collection with a new radiant depth of beauty and meaning. It will help you to intentionally choose gemstone colors to support your personal evolution. You can create a more satisfying and fulfilling environment by adding healthy, supportive gems and colors into your daily life.

Finally, living by Crystal Color Wisdom will help you navigate the rough waters of life with more flexibility and ease. The swift recognition of colors can help you make decisions, alert you to intuitive messages, and enable you to change course quickly and with confidence. I hope that living by Crystal Color Wisdom will not only brighten and lift your crystal practice, but will also enhance the quality and experience of your life.

HEALING COLORS GLOSSARY

Activating: Imbuing a gemstone with a specific intention or purpose in your crystal practice. This prepares the crystal for use in manifesting change and transformation.

Chakra: A swirling energy vortex within the energetic body. There are approximately 114 chakras distributed at specific physical locations in the body. They direct and manage the flow of energy and vitality throughout the energetic system.

Charging: The process of saturating a crystal with nourishing energy to enhance the effects of your crystal practice.

Cleansing: The practice of releasing accumulated energy from a gemstone so it can function and support you at an optimum level.

Crystal Energy: The vibrational and color energy that emits from the gemstone.

Crystal Healing: The practice of using crystals to support and aid in the healing process of body, mind, heart and spirit.

Crystal Wisdom: A process of using crystals and gemstones to tap into your own inner wisdom for support and guidance for your life situations.

Energy Body: The aspect of our body that is comprised of the vital energy of life. It consists of energy channels and centers that flow through our bodies as blood flows through our veins. Also known as the energetic body, energetic self or the aura.

Energy Work: Any system that channels, manipulates and directs the energy of our energetic body, environment, or external source. Examples of practices are Tai Chi, Qi Gong, yoga, acupuncture, breathing exercises, chakra balancing, and Reiki, to name a few.

Feng Shui: The art of optimizing energy flow within a person or environment by strategically arranging elements of the environment and intentional color choice.

Grounding: The act of connecting with the stable presence of the earth and bringing your attention to the present moment. This can also involve releasing excess energy into the ground to balance your own energy system.

Guardian Gemstones: A small collection of gemstones that are intentionally chosen to support you in releasing, healing, or cultivating specific aspects of your current life. See my book *Crystal Wisdom: Unearthing the Power of Gemstones for Positive Life Change* to learn how to select your Guardian Gemstones.

Highest Good: The most optimum and nourishing state of life. One in which we are living our daily life in concert with our spiritual goals and ideals.

Inner Guide: The aspect, presence, or voice, within you that provides you with truth and inner wisdom.

Inner Wisdom: The subconscious knowledge and truth you hold within you that aren't accessed via your thinking mind.

Intention: A purpose, quality, or goal that you are actively trying to cultivate and manifest in your life.

Intuition: The additional sense that collects and presents non-physical information not tangible to our five physical senses.

Manifesting: Actively planning and fostering a goal, project, state-of-mind or opportunity into your life. To take an idea from thought and dream to tangible reality.

Receiving Hand: Your nondominant hand. The hand you do not write with. This is the hand that receives the energy of the crystals.

Reiki: A healing practice that enables a practitioner to channel Reiki healing energy to themselves or to clients to aid in healing of the body, heart, mind, and spirit.

Releasing: The intentional act of letting go of overwhelming or excess energy or emotions. This is often accomplished during meditation. You can exhale and allow energy, tension, and overwhelming emotion to dissolve away on your breath.

Sending Hand: Your dominant hand. The hand you write with. This is the hand that sends out the energy of the crystals.

Synchronicity: When two things occur simultaneously and seem significant to each other but don't have a discernable connection to each other. One event didn't cause or influence the other event, they just occurred closely in time to each other. These are coincidences that seem very meaningful.

Wisdom: Information that is based on experience and knowledge that supports us in a positive manner.

REFERENCES

Abt, Thoedore. *Introduction to Picture Interpretation: According to C.G. Jung.* Switzerland: Living Human Heritage Publications, 2005.

Alcantara, Margarita. *Chakra Healing: A Beginner's Guide to Self-Healing Techniques that Balance the Chakras.* Berkley, CA: Althea Press, 2017.

Ashby, Nina. *Color Therapy Plain & Simple: The Only Book You'll Ever Need.* Charlottesville, VA: Hampton Roads, 2006.

Dale, Cyndi. *The Complete Book of Chakra Healing: Activate the Transformative Power of Your Energy Centers.* Woodbury, MN: Llewellyn Publications, 2009.

Eckstut, Joann & Eckstut, Arielle. *Secret Language of Color: Science, Nature, History, Culture, Beauty of Red, Orange, Yellow, Green, Blue, & Violet.* New York, NY: Black Dog & Leventhal Publishers, 2013.

Frazier, Karen. *Crystals for Healing: The Complete Reference Guide.* Berkley, CA: Althea Press, 2015.

Gardner, Joy. *Vibrational Healing Through the Chakras: With Light, Color, Sound, Crystals, and Aromatherapy.* Berkley, CA: Crossing Press, 2006.

Govinda, Kalashatra. *A Handbook of Chakra Healing: Spiritual Practice for Health, Harmony and Inner Peace.* Old Saybrook, CT: Konecky & Konecky, 2004.

Hall, Judy. *The Crystal Bible: A Definitive Guide to Crystals.* Cincinnati, OH: Walking Stick Press, 2003.

Hall, Judy. *The Crystal Bible 2.* Cincinnati, OH: Walking Stick Press, 2009.

Hall, Judy. *The Crystal Bible 3.* Blue Ash, OH: Walking Stick Press, 2013.

Haller, Karen. *The Little Book of Colour: How to Use the Psychology of Colour to Transform Your Life*. UK: Penguin Life, 2019.

Judith, Anodea. *Eastern Body, Western Mind: Psychology and the Chakra System As a Path to the Self*. Berkley, CA: Celestial Arts, 2004.

Judith, Anodea. *Wheels of Life: A User's Guide to the Chakra System*. Woodbury, MN: Llewellyn Publications, 1987.

Kastan, David & Farthing, Stephen. *On Color*. UK: Yale University Press, 2018.

Lewis, Richard G. *Color Psychology: Profit From The Psychology of Color: Discover the Meaning and Effects of Color*. Present Riana Publishing, 2014.

McLeod, June. *Colour Psychology Today*. UK: O-Books, 2016.

McLeod, June. *Colour of the Soul: Tranform Your Life Through Colour Therapy*. UK: O-Books, 2006.

Melody. *Love is in the Earth: A Kaleidoscope of Crystals*. Wheat Ridge, CO: Earth-Love Publishing House, 1995.

Mihalache, P. V. *Chromotherapy: Colours and Well-Being*. 2012.

Murphy, S. *Tumbled Stones Picture Book. Volume 13: Over 700 Stones by Color*. 2016.

Myss, Caroline. *Anatomy of the Spirit: The Seven Stages of Power and Healing*. New York, NY: Harmony Books, 1996.

Rossbach, Sarah & Yun, Lin. *Living Color: Master Lin Yuns Guide to Feng Shui and the Art of Color*. New York, NY: Kodansha America Inc. 1994.

Sawn-Foster, Nora. *Jungian Art Therapy: Images, Dreams, and Analytical Psychology*. New York: Routledge, 2018.

Simmons, Robert & Ahsian, Naisha. *The Book of Stones, Revised Edition: Who They Are and What They Teach*. Berkley, CA: North Atlantic Books, 2015.

Ter Maximus, Mercurius. *Color Symbolism: A Study of the Psychology and Meaning behind Colors*. Heill, 2018.

Valnet, Christian. *Chromotherapy: The power of colors*. Eizioni R.E.I., 2019.

Wolfgang von Goethe, Johann. *Theory of Colours*. Cambridge, Massachusetts: The MIT Press, 1970.

Wright, Angela. *Colour Affects*. http://www.colour-affects.co.uk/

Wright, Angela. *The Beginner's Guide to Colour Psychology*. UK: Kyle Cathie Limited, 1995.

ABOUT THE AUTHOR

SHANNON MARIE is supported in life by her husband, children, and their cuddly cats in a home full of gemstones. She has spent the last fifteen years creating gemstones jewelry, writing articles about crystals, and providing meditation and gemstone education videos on YouTube. After many years of informal study, Shannon completed the Certified Professional Gemologist training with the International Gem Society.

Shannon's extensive studies of therapeutic healing modalities began with a certification as a Reiki Master and Teacher in 2004. She then went on to obtain a Master's degree from the Institute of Transpersonal Psychology. Shannon completed a 200-hour Yoga Teacher Training course with Blue Lotus Yoga in North Carolina, followed by Practitioner Certification in Phoenix Rising Yoga Therapy. She has enjoyed deepening her meditation practice with her Buddhist teachers and Sangha at Dawn Mountain in Houston, Texas. Shannon combined her love and knowledge of gemstones with her broad scope of therapeutic training to create the transformative meditation practice of Crystal Wisdom.

ACKNOWLEDGMENTS

As always, I am most thankful for the love and support of my family. My husband and kids gave me the quiet and space to write, the necessary encouragement when I felt low, and the motivation to help me reach the finish line. I am fortified and strengthened by the love, reassurance, and enthusiasm of my family.

Thank you to my Mom who is my biggest fan and cheerleader. She has always been supportive of any endeavor I set my heart and mind to. Not everyone has parents that support them unconditionally, so I acknowledge and appreciate this beautiful gift. She is a blessing to me!

Thank you so much to my dear friend Hanh. She listened to and encouraged me as I enthused about "my book idea" during our regular walks and lunches. Although published second, this book was the very first I dreamed up. Being a published author was only the glimmer of a dream and Hanh motivated me to go for it!

I am so grateful to the friends in our author's group, Claire Villarreal, PhD, and Dent Gitchel, Jr. Regular meetings with these superb, creative, and spiritual people kept me accountable to my goals, excited about my current project, and provided new ideas and inspiration. They served as a vital community and kept me from feeling alone while swimming out in the ocean of book crafting.

Thank You Dear Reader!

Thank you for taking the time to learn about the powerful practice of working with Crystal Wisdom Colors. I feel honored that you have decided to explore this world of crystals and gemstones with me. I wish you all the best as you take your steps down the Crystal Wisdom path!

You can find continuing support at **www.Crystal-Wisdom.com** and at **https://www.youtube.com/c/ReikiGemWellness.**

Keep checking in there to learn about new books, online courses, and live workshops!

www.ingramcontent.com/pod-product-compliance
Lightning Source LLC
Chambersburg PA
CBHW040423100526
44589CB00022B/2806